How to Analyze People

...and Spur Them to Come Out of Their Shell.

A Practical Guide to Mastering Social Skills and
Understanding Body Language, Human Behavior and
Emotional Influence without Going Nuts.

By Ted Freedom

Table of Contents

Introduction

Non-verbal communication is critical in communication, and it is continual, unlike verbal communication. When silent, you are communicating. When body language contradicts verbal communication, body language is qualified over verbal communication and taken as the true state of the person. Non-verbal communication gives a hint about the emotional state of the person. For this reason, exhibiting the right communication skills and understanding communication accurately can improve communication as well as enhance life chances.

Some aspects of life that need analysis of people are parenting, teaching, talking therapy, and intimacy. Against this backdrop, this book offers the much-needed understanding and application of body language reading competencies for a novice and professional communicator.

Correspondingly, this book explored what constitutes human behavior as well as verbal communication. It is important to understand the dynamism of human behavior and verbal communication before delving into communication skills. We explored body language as eye contact, facial expressions, and gestures, among others.

Eye contact and touch in form handshake and hugs are repeatedly used in informal and formal communication setups. The ability to read all sets of communication cues such as voice, posture, and gestures is critical in initiating and sustaining effective communication as well as relationships. For parents, teachers, and psychotherapist, as well as criminal investigators, comprehensive understanding of non-verbal communication is a lifetime behavior.

We explored the full spectrum of analyzing people, including distance and space in communication and paralinguistic aspect of body language. Finally, the reader is guided on ways of enhancing communication skills, and finally, the reader is taken through ways of exploiting body reading skills to enhance acceptable social outcomes.

In addition, understanding body language, and non-verbal communication for that matter, enables the observer to analyze people. This is important insofar as understanding that the true motivations of a person are and what feelings lie behind the words of a person. Analyzing people can unlock the secrets of behavior especially when a person is trying their best to conceal their true intentions.

Furthermore, non-verbal communication can help decipher the state of mind that a person may find themselves in.

So, let's take a look at how analyzing people, and other forms of communication, can help you analyze the psychology behind a person.

Chapter 1:
Human Behavior Introduction

From a psychological viewpoint, human behavior concerns the full spectrum of emotional and physical behaviors that humans engage in that include social, biological and intellectual actions and are impacted by attitudes, culture, ethics, rapport, and genetics among other considerations. Human behavior is a complex interplay of cognition, actions, and emotion.

Correspondingly, actions are behavior as actions capture everything that can be observed. Actions can be captured through eyes or through physiological sensors. An initiation or transition from one state to another is an action. Actions as behaviors can happen at various time scales starting from muscular activation to sweat gland activity, sleep, or food consumption.

For cognition as behavior, cognition defines thoughts and mental images that one carries and can be both non-verbal and verbal. For instance, "I have to work on my book" can be treated as verbal cognition. On the other hand, imagine how your project will look after reworking on it is considered a non-verbal cognition.

As such, cognitions consist of skills and knowledge by knowing how to apply tools in a constructive manner such as memorizing the color of a jacket or singing songs.

When viewing emotions as behavior, emotions are considered as a relatively brief conscious experience marked by intense mental activity and a feeling that is not influenced by either knowledge or reasoning. Emotions normally happen from a positive to negative scale. Increased arousal can cause other aspects of physiology that are indicative of emotional processing, such as enhanced respiration rate. Emotions can only be inferred indirectly akin to cognition through monitoring facial expressions and tracking arousal, among others.

Understanding Behavior from a Psychological Viewpoint

Investment model

Human behavior can be understood in terms of work effort focused toward creating change. For instance, whether Hilda is headed out due to the need to watch the movie or wants to be with his boyfriend, the act of going to the movie is a form of investment. In this manner, human behavior occurs due to the need to get a particular outcome.

The return of this investment can be found from the movie Hilda watches or a kiss from his boyfriend at the end of it. In this aspect, behavior involves making consideration of the investment in terms of calories, time, risks, and opportunity costs.

The motivation of where to invest our actions to spur particular behavior to emanate from evolutionary influences that have made us prioritize sex, food, safety, territory, and higher social status over other states of affairs.

Genetics also impact certain behavioral traits, such as dispositions and temperaments. For instance, extroverted people find stimulating social situations more satisfying compared to introverted people.

Against this backdrop, the learning history of an individual impact the investment value system. For instance, if Hilda loved the first two Star Wars movies, then we expect her to show a strong desire to see the third.

An illustration of the investment model of human behavior is where one is sitting down watching television when an advert for apple pie activates in you the desire to get a cup of coffee. You have had a rough day, and you are not as fresh as you'd like to be. In your mind, a small computation takes place where you weigh on the value of getting up and getting a cup of coffee.

Eventually, your craving wins out, and you decide to go get a that cup of coffee. Unfortunately, a quick look in the cupboards indicates that there is no coffee which makes you take a glance of the trashcan where you notice the empty coffee tin.

Then feelings of irritation follow this interruption of your goal, and the thought briefly enters your mind to go to the store but your calculations that such a move would cost much time and effort makes you drop the idea. Finally, you settle on a glass of water with measured feelings of annoyance.

In detail, the investment model for understanding human behavior views behaviors in the form of the effort needed to realizing a particular outcome. The behavior costs in the form of time and energy computed in the form of benefits and costs. Human behavior is largely a cost-benefit analysis according to the investment model of animal behavior.

Most animal documentaries on the behavior of animals can help you realize how inherently animals make the cost-benefit analysis. Take the case of wildebeests in African savanna plains that need to drink water and cross the river that is infested with hungry crocodiles.

In this environment, water and grass are scarce, and wildebeests desperately need water and grass. At the same time, the wildebeests have to watch out for marauding crocodiles lurking under the surface of water ready to devour the wildebeests.

Eventually, wildebeests have to invoke an investment model of behavior to maximize the possibility of living, drinking water, and crossing the river to graze. Under this model, most wildebeests cautiously approach the river, ensuring that they near the river bank when drinking water which would enable them to retract sporadically at the slightest hint of danger.

In this manner, human behavior is a sort of commerce with the environment. The human being actions are primed to maximize benefits from the environment.

The mind is a critical component of behavior as it stores a history of what has desired outcomes as well as computing the cost-benefit analysis before one act. It can be argued that the investment model of behavior affirms the assumption that human behavior is conscious and well-thought.

Additionally, actions lead to lost opportunities, and one has to pursue an action that best maximizes the intended outcomes. For instance, if an animal spends time standing its ground, it is losing out on gathering resources for its survival.

Social influence model of human behavior
Human behavior can be viewed from the understanding that a human being is a social animal. Human behavior happens in the context of a social matrix. A social influence entails the actions that influence the investment of another person.

For instance, when Hilda was going to the movie, did she ask her boyfriend out or the boyfriend did ask her out. In most cases, social influence processes involve cooperation, cooperation, and whether the transactions move people closer or make them drift apart. Social influence also manifests as a resource. As a resource, social influence concerns the capacity to move other people in alignment with our interests.

Social influence in this context refers to the levels of social and respect value other people show us and the degree to which they listen, care about our well-being, and are willing to sacrifice for us. For instance, if Hilda is attracted to his boyfriend and he agrees to go to the movie with her, then this indicator that of social influence as a resource. If the boyfriend breaks up with Hilda is a potent indication of a loss of social influence.

Additionally, social influence is determined by the amount of attention from other people. In line with this understanding, the actions of a person will seek to attract attention from people or sustain the attention of people. Probably you have colleagues or public figures that consistently act to attract and sustain admiration from other people. At a personal level, one is likely to act in a manner that invites admiration from colleagues, friends, and other people. The behavior and likely behavior of an individual is likely to optimize admiration from others.

Furthermore, within the social influence model of human behavior, people are likely to act in a manner that invites more positive emotions than negative emotions from others. In a way, the need to attract more positive emotions from others is related to attracting admiration from others, but it is highly related to emotional intelligence. One can only enhance the likelihood of getting a positive emotional reaction from others if he or she has requisite emotional intelligence levels. Through emotional intelligence, one learns to show empathy and pay attention to how others are feeling. Against this backdrop, human behavior is likely to be reactive of how others are feeling, or it is likely to be highly considerate of others for the motivation of attracting positive emotions from them.

Then there is the degree to which others will sacrifice their interests for the sake of another person as a mark of social influence. People with strong social influence will have tens to thousands of people willing to sacrifice their interests for the sake of the person. The behavior of the individual with strong social influence is likely to take into account that there are tens to thousands of people are willing to forego their interests for the sake of the influential figure. On the other hand, the followers of the influential people are likely to take the actions of the individual as guidance or message of how one should act and live.

Justification model of human behavior

First, human behavior requires justifications by legitimizing it. For instance, when you shout at someone, there are chances that one will qualify the behavior by stating that they were upset. In reaching justification, one assesses the behavior and the ideal outcome.

For instance, the ideal outcome may have been attracting admiration from others, but one ended up embarrassing themselves in public. Expectedly, the individual will feel angry for not only failing to attain ideal reaction from the audience but also degrading the status quo. In this state, the individual will justify subsequent undesired behavior by drawing attention to the disappointment he or she got earlier on.

Using the Hilda and the movie example, Hilda may have felt justified to make her boyfriend tag along to the movie and allow the boyfriend to show romance because of this what lovers do.

The justification of her behavior and the boyfriend's behavior emanates from observation and learned patterns of what lovers do and not necessarily of how each of them individually feels.

Justification of behavior can be simply that is what others do, and so the individual is obliged to emulate the same. Try watching court proceedings for you to realize how people place significant value of justification for their behavior.

At the corporate level, organizations have invested significantly in assessing human behavior during recruitment stages and as well as assessing workers. Human behavior is complex, and organizations seek to have the best bet in recruiting and retaining fairly predictable workers.

Most of the personality tests administered during hiring and appraisal processes are meant to help profile workers and have a predictable look at how each of the workers may behave. There have been attempts to determine a formula for human behavior as a simple system, but it has been satisfactorily concluded that human behavior is dynamic.

Reading personality types

In general terms, most people fall into one of these four personality types. Of course, there are individuals who have issues in which they may not fall into these categories. Nevertheless, the vas majority of people will fall into one of these four groups:

- **Average.** This is the most common personality type. This is a range in which all of the aspects of a person fall into average ranges. For example, they score average in areas such as openness, introversion, neuroticism, pessimism, and so on. These are people who test at normal levels for sociability, self-control, responsiveness and aggression.

- **Reserved.** These folks score average in most areas. The main difference is that they have low levels of neuroticism but high levels of agreeableness, introversion, and consciousness. They folks are very stable emotionally. These are people who tend to be a bit more quiet, less sociable and may deal with higher levels of anxiety as compared to other personality types.

- **Role models.** These are folks who are natural leaders. They have high levels of agreeableness, extraversion, openness and interpersonal people skills. Natural leaders tend to be more optimistic, active and outgoing. The are much less prone to aggression though they may exhibit more protective instincts. They also have a high degree of self-control.

- **Self-centered.** These are individuals who score high in extraversion, but rank lower in agreeableness and interpersonal relationships. They tend to be more focused on their own needs as opposed to role models. Their levels of impulsiveness, restlessness and pessimism might test a bit higher than normal.

Based on the four broad models, reading people becomes an important part of having healthy and effective personal relationships. The main thing to keep in mind is that your interpersonal relationships will be affected by your ability to communicate effectively. And this begins with recognizing what your interlocutor is trying to tell you.

Of course, there are cases in which some people are not completely encompassed into these categories. But in general terms, most people with whom you communicate will fall into one of these categories. As such, you can quickly recognize who you are dealing with and then adjust your communication strategy accordingly.

Furthermore, understanding these personality types is rooted in understanding the needs of humans. In this case, Maslow's hierarchy of needs provides a great way of visualizing the needs of people. Here is an explanation of this model:

- **Physiological needs.** The first level of needs are basic physiological needs such as air, water, food, shelter, and health. These are the needs that all humans must have in order to ensure survival of the species.

- **Safety needs.** These needs are rooted in personal safety, job security, resources and private property. These are needs which help individuals feel safe in their environment.

- **Love and belonging.** These are personal and interpersonal needs which are met by having interrelations with other humans. They fill core psychological and emotional needs.

- **Esteem.** These are personal needs focused on self-esteem, status, reputation, recognition, and so on. These are the types of needs that people must fulfill in order to feel happy.

- **Self-actualization.** The final step is achieving the status that you dream for yourself. In other words, you are at a level in which you feel completely fulfilled and satisfied with yourself.

By understanding these needs, you can get a clear picture on what motivates and drives people. Needless to say, if people's basic needs are met, they will have the opportunity to focus more on belonging, esteem and self-actualization.

This is something critical when it comes to communication as these needs will provide additional influence on the way your interlocutor's will transmit information to you.

So, do take the time to become familiar with these types of needs so that you can focus on what types of needs people focus on in their daily lives.

Chapter 2:
Verbal Communication

Verbal communication involves both written and verbalized communication. Most people largely think of verbal communication as only talking. The main aspect of verbal communication is the use of words to encode a message. Verbal communication will include written speeches and spoken speeches.

Diction

The diction refers to the choice of words and how they are spoken. The choice of words tells more about communication. In a broad sense, the choice of words differentiates between formal and informal communication contexts. In the formal communication settings, the words used are standard, respectful, and diplomatic. An individual that tends to relapse into using standard and respectful language when communicating in grapevine communication is likely to be a professional or well-cultured person. Grapevine communication is likely to communicate more about the sex, ethnicity, and age of the person as it is an informal communication devoid of strict demands of corporate communication.

For this reason, when listening to someone, it is important to pay attention to how they approach controversial and emotive issues during the conversation. Try to listen to phrases like "I find that disturbing versus I think that is awkward," "Unfortunately I cannot agree with that versus I flatly decline" and many others. Try to reflect on friends and colleagues that tend to sound formal even when having a casual conversation. You will notice that most of them are schooled and probably working in formal employment.

In most cases, people will use region-specific, sex-specific, and race-specific words that can give away their demographic profile. While purposely leaving out non-verbal aspects of communication, the words we use will easily indicate our ethnicity, religion, age, and sex. During grapevine or casual communication, an individual is likely to use words and phrases that denote their biases, prejudice, and beliefs on various aspects of life. For instance, the words and phrases you use when with your clique watching a game or partying is likely to truly capture your personal beliefs and biases on life.

Additionally, the choice of words informs more about the work of an individual. Vocabulary is highly contextual, and this makes it easier to determine the nature of work that an individual does. When having a conversation with an information technologist at one point, you will realize that the individual uses technological analogies and illustrations to explain things. At one point when having a conversation with a stranger, you quickly figured out the likely profession of the person from certain words that the person used. For instance, without having prior knowledge, one is likely to guess that the person they are speaking to is an attorney, environmentalist, or a nurse. The choice of words that we use is likely to give away our professions.

Correspondingly, the choice of words can tell of the emotional status of the person speaking. Apart from non-verbal communication, verbal communication is adequate to give a preview of our mental status with respect to our emotions. When one is angry or disappointed, then he or she is likely to use cuss words as well as insults. One is also likely to speak a lot of words than usual when upset. On the contrary, one is likely to speak an average number of words and use words that do not elicit intense emotions when speaking and when feeling calm. Think of the choice of words that you use when your favorite team loses a game and when the team wins a game.

Transitional phrases

When speaking, transition words help us to show how one block of communication is connecting to another. When denoting an addition, we use phrases such as in addition to, secondly, or furthermore, among others. Transition phrases denoting addition suggest more information and more evidence.

The role of transition phrases is to help the listener follow the blocks of messages being exchanged to make a connection and get the full picture. While transition phrases appear basic language constructs, they reveal a lot when analyzing a report or a confession. It is through transition words that investigators get hints of a new perspective of an ongoing case.

Another important class of transition words is contradictions. Contradictory words include phrases like, however, but, apart from and on the contrary among others.

Contradictory words help provide the opposing view of what has been presented. Among the transition phrases, contradictory words purposely introduce the new viewpoint that is mostly opposing what has been presented.

Contradictory phrases challenge assumptions and known positions. When listening to someone, pay attention to any contradictory words which give information that was not provided before. In some cases, contradictory phrases are meant to prepare the room for failure or less ambitious outcomes.

For instance, "I will prepare the report through the internet has been slow for the most part of this week." From this statement, the contradictory word "though" serves to prepare the audience for the negative outcome as much as they await a positive outcome.

Equally important is that transitional words are used to emphasize a point during communication. Words that denote emphasis include for emphasis, again and to underscore among other transition words. Transition words that emphasize are meant to draw focus on certain aspects of the message that are deemed high value.

When someone uses phrases that emphasize then the person is trying to say that the particular aspect of the message is critical and should be remembered and acted upon. For instance, "Again, I would like you to do a summary of chapter one." The transition word, again, is a continuous reminder to the audience to attach criticality to the need to make a summary of chapter one.

Additionally, transition phrases help us to make comparisons. Transition words that denote comparison include similarly, by the same measure, and akin among others. The role of these phrases is to announce that the speaker or writer is now juxtaposing what has been presented before to what is being presented right now.

At an advanced level, an individual that uses comparative phrases may be narcissistic or may be suffering from low self-esteem. While the use of transition phrases appears as merely connecting ideas, it may speak more about the personality of an individual.

Narcissistic individuals have a false sense of self-importance and would seize any opportunity to compare themselves against others where they always emerge as the best.

Activity

Log in to Facebook and search a random person that you know not. If the person's profile is not public, look for another random person whom you can access and read their status. Once you access the profile, read the timeline, where he or she posts status, for the last fifteen recent statuses written by the individual. Focus on text status only.

Try to scan for transition phrases and words that denote emotions from the status. From the status; try to guess the personality of the individual and what they are going through.

There are high chances that from a simple analysis of the text status of anyone on Facebook, one is likely to guess their profession, emotional status, and personality. At the end of this exercise, remember to delete the search history and understand this exercise was for learning purposes and that you do not have express legal permission to analyze Facebook users.

Verbal communication in terms of privacy levels

Intrapersonal communication

The communication that happens within us, such as monologues or speaking to no one constitutes intrapersonal communication. For instance, when you interrogate yourself loudly or assure yourself loudly, "I can," then this is intrapersonal verbal communication. Intrapersonal verbal communication can also happen where you scream at yourself" Boy, I am a letdown, why?" In intrapersonal verbal communication, one is fully aware that they are speaking to inner self and voice it.

Intrapersonal verbal communication is different from speaking to an inanimate object. Most people speak to themselves only that they do not verbalize it.

Interpersonal communication

It is a form of communication that happens between two individuals. For instance, when you are talking to a classmate, then you are having an interpersonal communication. In interpersonal communication, emotional intelligence is important as the communicators need assurance that the other person is listening and understanding as well as relating to the message. Interpersonal communication is relative communication as it requires adjusting the communication to accommodate the other person.

The participants frequently switch between sender and receiver role. When done physically, most of the interpersonal communication happens within close distance.

Small group communication

It is communication involving more than two people and but less than a large gathering. In simple terms, the audience does not require the speaker to shout or use a public address system.

In group communication, many of the participants are allowed to interact and mingle with the rest. The participants take turns to speak and may interrupt the conversation at any point.

A small group communication requires social skills such as leadership, conflict management, and cultural competence to make everyone feel comfortable and appreciated.

For instance, through persuasion and influencing skills, one will find public social space not only approachable but fulfilling. The art of showing enthusiasm in other individuals and convincing them to buy into your ideas is known as persuasion. Persuasive or influential people will read the emotional currents in a situation and perfect what they are saying to appeal to spur involved.

Persuasion is a function of communication and personality, and this demands that you become an effective communicator who is empathetic to others. Winning over people requires trying to convince them to join your course. One must learn to sell your views as a salesperson would do.

As indicated, leadership is critical in all aspects of social interactions and in resolving conflicts. Against this backdrop, emotional intelligence and leadership skills are connected in multiple ways. The ability to influence requires that you tune your emotions and those of others to win them over. Influence is a critical attribute of good leadership.

It is sometimes called charisma, but though leadership skills involving influence goes beyond charisma to align with good emotional intelligence. The competencies of good leadership require you to articulate a vision and those other people with it. One does not have to be in a formal leadership position to exhibit leadership.

While holding your colleagues accountable, support, and direct their performance. Aspire to learn to lead by example

Public communication
When one addresses a large gathering of people, then it becomes public communication. Public communication requires preparation and research on the demographics of the audience.

Expectedly, cultural competence is important as audiences are diverse and sensitive to religious affiliation, ethnicity, sexual orientation, and gender.

Public communication requires formal language and explicit use of transitional phrases to help the audience connect. The language used in communication should be free of jargons.

Chapter 3:
Non-verbal Communication

In this context, non-verbal communication refers to body language. Starting with facial expressions, the human face is highly expressive and conveys countless emotions even without verbalizing anything. Fortunately, non-verbal communications are standard as the facial expressions for happiness, anger, sadness, and fear are the same across cultures.

Like most aspects of non-verbal communication, one has little control on the source and manifestation of facial expression, making it a critical aspect of evaluating the honesty of communication. From facial expressions, we can determine how one is feeling.

In subsequent chapters, we will detail how one can read facial expressions and other types bodily communication.

Then there is body movement and posture. How one stands, sits, holds their head, or walks affects how one is perceived by others. For instance, our posture communicates much about our attentiveness and eagerness when listening to a speech. Our posture also communicates our emotional status.

If one is angry, then they are unlikely to appear composed, and they are likely to stand upright for long or slouch for long. When one is excited, he or she is likely to change posture and movements frequently than when one feels sad. Recall when you felt highly excited, you probably walked fast, jumped, sat, and stood up frequently than usual.

Another form of non-verbal communication is gestures. Hand gestures are used to beckon, wave, point, or direct. In most cases, hand gestures happen without much intervention from the conscious mind. The meaning of most hand gestures varies across cultures. An innocent message created by a hand gesture in one country may be offensive in another country.

We can read the emotional status of an individual from their hand gestures even if they speak contrary. For instance, when one is angry, he or she is likely to throw their hands in the air in an uncoordinated manner. In most instances, hand gestures contradict verbal communication, especially where one is feeling emotional and tries to mask it.

Correspondingly, there is eye contact, which is a critical component of body language. The way one looks at another person during communication indicates hostility, affection, interest, and confidence. Individuals that have difficulties initiating and sustaining eye contact are largely considered as shy.

When one feels embarrassed, he or she is likely not to make and sustain eye contact. Prolonged eye contact at a particular person or groups of people is a stare and indicates judgment. Think of how your teacher looked at you when you were talking while others were writing. Prolonged eye contact is used to judge and intimidate. In the subsequent chapters, we will explore eye contact in detail.

Another critical aspect of body language is touch. A lot of meaning is attached to touch, and in some cases, touch impacts the development of a person. In the formative years, children need touch, reassuring fondle to feel secure and loved.

In fact, psychologists can determine bonding issues where one of the parents shows reluctance to touch and fondle their kid. For adults, touch manifests commonly as a handshake and a hug.

A firm handshake denotes confidence and familiarity while a weak handshake suggests a lack of confidence and unfamiliarity. A hug serves the same role as a handshake, but hugs for individuals in love may be prolonged.

Equally important, there is space as part of non-verbal communication. Getting too close to the person you are having communication with will make them uncomfortable unless it is in exceptional situations. For lovers trying to connect more with each other, getting closer to each other may sound romantic.

In teaching, there is what they call the professional distance, which is the standard distance allowable between a teacher and the student when communicating. When someone gets too close, then the other person may feel suffocated, trapped, and intimidated. Getting too far is also counterproductive as it makes the other person strain to participate in the communication.

Then there is a voice as part of non-verbal communication. How loud we speak denotes emphasis. The pace of our speaking captures our emotional status. Speaking fast may indicate that one has panicked or one is feeling insecure and wants to get through with speaking as fast as they can.

The tone and inflection of the voice tell more about the attitude of the speaker and the nature of the message.

For instance, the message may sound standard and devoid of emotions, but the tone and pitch of the speaker may bring out excitement or temper. The tone of the speaker may indicate anger or sarcasm.

Even though non-verbal communication can be manipulated or faked, it is difficult to manipulate all forms of non-verbal communication in one episode. It is not possible to fake tone, gestures, touch, distance, and facial expressions to align with verbal communication.

For this reason, body language remains a strong source of reading and ascertaining the emotional status of an individual. Nevertheless, it is possible to learn and exert control over your body language to enhance particular outcomes. Just like we learn to guide our emotions and subsequent reactions, we can exert more control over contextual clues.

There is also a possibility of receiving confusing non-verbal communication which is unintentionally sent by the source. In most cases, a confusing non-verbal communication harms relationships. At one point you might have smile unintentionally only for your friend to think you are celebrating their losses.

Illustrations of non-verbal communication perceptions

Richard

Richard believes that he gets along well with his colleagues at work, but if you question any of the colleagues, they think that Richard is intimidating and very intense. Most of the friends think that Richard eye contact is a stare that seeks to devour others through the eyes.

Richard's colleagues are of the view that if he takes your hand, he lunges to grab it and then squeeze so hard that it hurts. Richard is a caring lad who wishes that he attracted more friends, but his non-verbal language keeps people at a distance and constraints his ability to advance at work.

Sharon

Sharon is elegant and is outgoing and has no qualms meeting eligible men but she has a hard time maintaining a relationship for longer than a few months, Sharon is social and interesting but exhibits tension even though she constantly smiles and laughs.

Her voice is shrill, shoulders and eyebrows are noticeably raised, and the body is stiff.

Most people around Sharon feel anxious and uncomfortable, and it is this discomfort from people that makes Sharon feels unease with her life.

Solomon

Even though Solomon thought that he had found the perfect match when he met Alice, Alice was not so certain. Solomon is good looking, a smooth talker, and hardworking but seemed to care about his thoughts than those of Alice.

When Alice had something to speak, Solomon was always read with judging eyes and a rebuttal before she could finish her thought. All these developments made Alice feel ignored, and soon, she started showing interest in other men. The inability of Solomon to listen to others makes him unpopular with many of the individuals he most admires.

All these smart and well-intentioned people struggle in their attempt to socialize with others. The unfortunate thing is that they are unaware of the body language they communicate. If one wants to communicate effectively, they should avoid misunderstandings and enjoy a trusting relationship, both professionally and socially. One should understand how to use and interpret body language and enhance their non-verbal communication.

Perhaps the most challenging and most valuable aspect of non-verbal communication is that it is happening even when one is not initiating. For this reason, body language can be frustrating, especially where one is trying to mask something while the non-verbal communication keeps on giving them away.

At some point, you have been in a relationship and detected lies from your partner despite the best attempts by your partner to cover their trails. On the other hand, non-verbal communication provides the most dependable indicator of the status of an individual even when the person is attempting to mask their true status.

Correspondingly, most people feel frustrated by non-verbal communication because they cannot always control it even with rehearsals. Think of trying to assure your partner that you are not offended, but the tone and pitch of your voice suggest that you are upset. The listener will feel that you are not being honest with yourself and to the listener. It is important to align verbal communication with non-verbal communication and not the other way round.

When reading people, try to pay attention to inconsistencies exhibited by the communicator. Usually, non-verbal communication should reinforce verbal communication. Where inconsistencies manifest, then the individual is trying to mask their true emotional status. It is important to analyze non-verbal communication signals as a group rather than a single non-verbal cue. For instance, analyze the tone of the voice, facial reactions, hand gestures and visual contact a group of related components.

It is essential to remember that some individuals are born with conditions that make them appear to show inconsistencies when communicating non-verbally, but they are honest in their communication. For instance, they are people born shy due to parental issues that make them shy off when interacting with people. A shy person will have challenges in initiating and sustaining eye contact, and this has nothing to do with their emotional status and honesty of their verbal message.

There are individuals born with hyperhidrosis, which is a condition that makes them sweat excessively even when the weather is cold and with no strenuous movement. The hands and feet of such people sweat, and they will avoid handshakes or eye contact, which should not be interpreted as panicking, insecurity, and anxiety.

Chapter 4:

Eye Contact

Reading eye contact is important to understand the true status of an individual even where verbal communication seeks to hide it. As advised, body language should be read as a group, but in this chapter and subsequent chapters, we will focus on individual aspects of non-verbal communication and make the reader understand how to read that particular type of non-verbal cues.

Starting with pupils, the pupil dilates when one is interested in the person they are talking to or the item we are looking at. The pupils will contract when one is transiting from one topic to another. We have no control over the working of pupils. When one is speaking about a less interesting topic, the pupils will contract.

Effective eye contact is critical when communicating with a person. Eye contact implies that one looks but does not stare. Persistent eye contact will make the recipient feel intimidated or judged. In Western cultures, regular eye contact is desired, but it should not be overly persistent. If one offers constant eye contact, then it is seen as an attempt to intimidate or judge, which makes the recipient of the eye contact uncomfortable.

There are studies that suggest that most children are prone to attacks by pets if their visual contact is constantly regular, that makes them to feel as they were in danger and defensive. Initiating an insistent visual contact is a sign of an individual's heightened awareness of the messages they are being transmitted. Lying can be detected by the individual avoiding visual contact.

Evasive eye contact

Having evasive eye contact is a mark of uneasiness. We try not to look at a person if we feel embarrassed to be communicating at them. When we feel shameful about trying to fool people, we avoid looking at them. While it is okay to blink or drop eye contact temporarily, people that consistently shun making eye contact are likely to be feeling uneasy with the message or the person they are communicating with.

For emphasis, staring at someone will make them drop eye contact due to feeling intimidated. Evasive eye contact happens where one deliberately avoids making eye contact.

Crying

Human beings cry due to feeling uncontrollable pain or in an attempt to attract sympathy from others. Crying is considered as an intense emotion associated with grief or sadness though it can also denote extreme happiness known as tears of joy.

When an individual forces tears to fool others, then it is referred to as crocodile tears which imply faking tears to deceive others. If one cries then the individual is likely experiencing intense negative emotion.

Blinking

In most cases, blinking is instinctive, and our emotions and reactions directed to our interlocutor to whom we are speaking to can lead us to subconsciously alter our amount of blinking.

If the average rate of blinking is 6 to 9 instances per minute, then it is a strong indication that an individual is drawn to their interlocutor with whom they are speaking, and it is indicative of flirting. In normal contexts, men and women blink the same amount of times.

Winking

In Western culture, winking is considered as a form of flirting which should be done to people we are in good terms with. There are cross-cultural similarities with regard to winking. In Asian contexts, winking as a form of facial expressions is frowned upon.

Eye direction

The direction of the eyes tells us about how an individual is feeling. When someone is thinking, they tend to look to their left when they are recalling or reminiscing.

An individual that is thinking tends to look to the right when searching for creative ideas and it can be taken as an indicative sign of an individual trying to be deceitful in some instances such as creating a depiction of events.

For left-handed people, the eye directions will be reversed. Additionally, when one is interested in what you are speaking, he or she will make eye contact often.

Some studies have found that when people are taking part in an engaging conversation, then their eyes stay fixated on the face of their interlocutor, about 80% of the interaction but not wholly making visual contact. Rather the eye contact on the eyes of the other person is for the duration of 2-3 minutes then continue to the lips or nose then back up to the eyes. For a brief moment, the person initiating eye contact will look down then back up to make visual contact.

Looking back up to the right demonstrates dismissal and boredom. Dilation of the pupil may indicate that someone is interested or that the room is brighter.

In some instances, sustained eye contact may be a signal that you want to speak to the person or that you are interested in the person sexually. At one point, you have noticed a hard stare from a man towards a particular woman to the point the woman notices and asks the man what is all that for. In this case, eye contact is not being used to intimidate but to single out the target person. You probably have seen a woman ask why is that man staring at me then she proceeds to mind her business but on taking another look at the direction of the man the stare is still there.

In this manner, eye contact is used to single out an individual and make them aware that one is having sexual feelings towards the person.

However, people are aware of the impact of body language and will seek to portray the expected behaviors. For instance, an individual that is lying is likely to make deliberate eye contact frequently to sound believable.

At one point, you knew you were lying but went ahead to make eye contact. You probably have watched movies where one of the spouses is lying but makes believable eye contact with others. The reason for this faked body language is because the person is aware of the link between making eye contact and speaking the truth.

Like verbal language, non-verbal communication and in particular, eye contact can be highly contextual. For instance, an individual may wink to indicate that he or she agrees with the quality of the product being presented or that he or she agrees with the plan.

Eye contact in these settings can be used as a coded language for a group of people. At one point, one of your classmates may have used a wink to indicate that the teacher is coming or to indicate that the secret you have been guarding is now out.

Activity

1. Go through your laptop or movie collection and skip to instances where a couple or lovers are quarreling and pay attention to their eye contact. Where possible, pick a movie or TV series that you are yet to watch and scan through until where there is a scene of a couple or lovers quarreling and pay attention to their eye contact.

    For instance, pick any episode of the Game of Thrones and find any instance where people are quarreling or arguing. They need not be love scenes. Pay attention to their eye contact and try to summarize their eye contact and any other aspect of eye contact as non-verbal communication. What did you conclude from the eye contact of the select characters?

2. If you are certain that your lover can handle it, try initiating a false accusation that he or she is planning to move out of the country and then act the part. While in the discussion or quarrel, try to pay attention to eye contact of your lover and discover what you can conclude.

    For this exercise, the topic should only be "trying to move out of the country" and no other topic. You should not introduce any other topic.

At the end of the exercise debrief the lover by making them understand that it was a prank and a learning experience of body language and proceed to make them know the role of non-verbal communication.

3. Try observing children, especially when they cry. Do you think each crying episode of a child is genuine? Why or why not? How did you arrive at this conclusion? Have you felt manipulated by tears of a child or another person?

4. Assuming that you have a robust relationship with your friends or classmates, try staring hard at one of your classmate, especially the opposite sex. When he or she looks the other way, do not drop your stare. What was the eventual reaction of the person you were staring at?

Chapter 5:
Facial Expressions

As indicated, facial expressions should be interpreted among the entire set of body language, but in this chapter, we will detail how to read facial expressions. Wrinkles convey the intensity of emotions and the degree of originality of the emotion.

In most cases, wrinkles convey hardship and suffering as well as extreme anger. Wrinkles indicate that one is always smiling, senile, or nasty.

Facial expressions and emotions are related. Facial expressions can create an emotional experience. Smiling tends to induce more pleasant moods while frowning induces negative moods.

In this manner, facial gestures may produce emotion by creating physiological shifts in the body. Through the process of self-perception, people assume that they ought to be sad or happy because they are showing signs such as a smile or frown, and these cause emotion. Emotions are caused by other factors beyond facial expressions. For instance, emotions are largely a function of the human system of beliefs and stored information.

In other terms, you feel angry when you score less than average marks because the current system equates that to not being smart enough and the stored information reminds you that you risk repeating the test or not securing plum employment position and this entire make you feel hopeless, upset and stressed. There is a possibility that if the belief system did not deem less than average as a failure and the stored information shows a positive outlook for a such a score that you will feel happy or excited by the score.

Additionally, twitching your mouth randomly; either way indicates that one is deliberately not listening or degrading the importance of the message. The facial gesture is realized by closing the lips and randomly twitching the mouth to either the right or left akin to swirling the mouth with mouthwash.

The facial expression is also to indicate outright disdain to the speaker or the message. The facial expression is considered a rude way of expressing disgust with the speaker or the message and should be avoided at all cost.

Where one shuts their lips tightly, then it indicates the individual is feeling angry but does not wish to show the anger. Shutting the lips tightly may also indicate that the person is feeling unease but struggling to concentrate at all costs.

The source of the discomfort could be the immediate neighbors, the message, or the speaker. Through this gesture, the individual is indicating that he or she simply wants the speaker to conclude the speech because not all people are enjoying the message.

When one is angry or strongly disapproves what the speaker is saying, then the person will grin. A grin indicates that the person is feeling disgusted by what is being said.

In movies or during live interviews you probably so the interviewee grin when an issue or a person that the person feels is disgusting is mentioned. Showing a grin indicates that one harbors a strong dislike for the message or the speaker.

A person that is feeling uncomfortable due to sitting on a hard chair, a poorly ventilated room, or sitting next to a hostile neighbor may also show a grin which is not necessarily related to the message.

If one is happy, then one is likely to have a less tense face and a smile. Positive news and positive emotions are manifested as a smile or a less tense facial look. On the other hand if one is processing negative emotions, then the face of the person is likely to be tensed up due to exerting pressure on the body muscles.

A genuine smile like when one is happy is wide by average curve and is temporary. A prolonged smile that is very wide suggests that the individual is smirking at the message or the speaker. A prolonged smile may also suggest the individual is faking the emotion.

By the same measure, a frozen face may indicate intense fear. For instance, you have seen terrified faces when attending a health awareness forum on sexually transmitted diseases or some medical condition that terrified the audience.

In this setting, the face of the audience will appear as if it has been paused. The eyes and the mouth may remain stationary as the speaker presents the scary aspects of the medical condition. It appears negative emotions may slow down the normal conscious and unconscious movement of the muscles of the face.

In overall, human beings can identify facial expressions of about roughly six emotions with significant exactness. These include fear, happiness, disdain, surprise, and disgust. However, the universality and accuracy of facial expressions hold where it is a still image of an emotion.

The accuracy of such appreciations rises when people are permitted to make an assessment of the facial gesture in action. Due to the generalizations of facial expression, it can be concluded that they are inherent rather than learned actions. It has been observed that individuals with visual impairment produce similar facial expressions to people who are visually capable.

Aside from the cultural similarities, differences in facial expression of feelings happen throughout the world. One, people are likely to correctly interpret the facial expression of people from their culture compared to those of other cultures.

Nevertheless, people are still accurate in their assessment of people from other cultural groups. The appropriateness of facial expressions varies among subcultures of the same cultural group. Compared to the Japanese, Americans readily manifest anger, and this shows that individuals express emotion differentially across cultures.

If you are a teacher or trainer, then you encounter facial expressions from your students frequently. Assuming that you are a teacher, then you have noticed facial expressions indicating shock, uneasiness, and disapproval when you announce tests or indicate that the scores are out.

Form these facial expressions; you will concur that the students feel uncomfortable, uncertain, and worried. The students will show lines of wrinkles, look down, eyes wide open and mouths agape when sudden and uncomfortable news is announced. Even though the students may indicate that they are prepared for the test, their facial expressions suggest otherwise.

Like all forms of communications, effective reading of facial expressions will happen where the target person is unaware that you are reading even though they understand that their facial expressions are integral of the overall communication.

In other terms, when one becomes aware that he or she is being studied than the person will act in an expected manner or simply freeze expected reaction. It is akin to realizing that someone is feeling you.

Since the underlying emotion affects the facial expression that one shows. As indicated, the body language overrides verbal communication, which helps reveal the true status of an individual. One possible argument of the non-verb communication triumphing over verbal communication could be because the body prioritizes its physiological needs over other needs.

The physiological needs are critical to the survivability of an individual. Over centuries the human body could have been programmed to increase survivability rate by prioritizing physiological needs. Body language largely indicates the physiological state of an individual, which is meant to help the individual and others respect the true physiological status of the person.

Imagine what could happen where one is sickly, and it is worsening, but the person manages to manifest convincing body language of happiness and enthusiasm. The outcome would be prioritizing the emotional needs of the individual over the physiological needs.

Apart from laboratory tests and physical examination, it would be difficult for other people to realize that something is amiss and ask the individual to take rest. Without illness, when one feels anxious about the audience, then he or she manifests disharmony of the physiological status, and there is a necessity to make the person and the audience aware that the individual is suffering and that they should be understanding of the individual.

Chapter 6:

Gestures

Akin to the previous chapter, gestures should be interpreted in the context of other aspects of body language, but in this chapter, we will explore ways or reading gestures. We all talk with our hands often. For some people, the gesturing matches their message well. Some people do not deploy hand gestures while others overuse hand gestures. Most hand gestures are universal.

A person that does not use hand gestures may be perceived as indifferent. For this reason, the audience may feel that one does not care about what the other is talking about. If your hands are hidden, then the audience will find it difficult to trust you. If one's hands are open and the palms at a 45-degree angle, then the individual is communicating that he or she is being honest and open.

Notably, randomly throwing hands in the air while talking may indicate that anxiety or panic. Extreme anger will also make one throw their hands in an uncoordinated manner.

Take time and watch movie characters quarreling, and you will note that most people being accused of something will throw their hands in the air randomly. It is something that they have little control over.

Randomly throwing hands in the air indicates that one is overwhelmed with emotions or that one has given up defending their position in the argument and have left the argument to the individual that initiated.

Furthermore, one may point at a person or an object. Pointing as a gesture helps direct the focus of the speaker and the audience to the focused area. During your school days, you probably saw your teacher point in a particular direction without speaking until the students that were talking had to stop.

In this context, pointing at particular students drew the attention of the entire class to their direction, making them become the center of attention, and they had to do a quick self-evaluation and stop talking.

Relatedly, pointing while wafting the index finger indicates a warning. When you point your index finger at someone and waft it up and down, then you are denoting a strong warning and judgment to the individual.

It is the equivalent of saying, "you or this is the last warning." Probably your parent or teacher may have a point and waft gesture to signal a warning that what you are doing is wrong and that you should stop. In movie characters, you might have seen the police or the lead actor use the index finger to warn someone.

Additionally, spreading all the fingers and holding them together against those of the opposite hand indicates strong personal reflection, such as when praying or remembering the departed soul.

The same gesture may be used when one is focusing the mind during meditation or yoga. The holding of each of your fingers against their peers of the other hand may also indicate feeling humble and thankful of everything. Adherents of the Catholic faith frequently use this gesture when praying. The gesture indicates humility and thankfulness.

Then there is also the one of gently tapping on the head once or continuously. When one taps on the head using a hand or a finger, it indicates the individual is thinking hard or trying hard to recall something.

For instance, when speaking and you try to remember what another person said you might use this gesture. Children often tap their heads once or continuously using one finger or the entire palm to signal attempts to recall something. The gesture is the equivalent of saying, "come on what was it or come on what was the name again!"

Sometimes the gesture is simple and straightforward. A single raised finger, while others are folded, may indicate number one or the first item. Two raised fingers while the others are folded may indicate number two or the second item in the mentioned list. The same is true for the third, fourth, or fifth raised fingers.

Correspondingly, a fully raised palm with fingers spread may indicate that one should stop. When stopping the vehicle on the roadside, one raises one of their palms high up, and it is taken as a sign to stop. The same is true in the sporting context were raising one palm high up commonly communicates that the playing should stop. When arguing with your partner, if he or she raises one of their palms, then it is signaling the other to stop arguing or doing what he or she was doing.

Additionally, clapping the palms together may indicate applauding the message or the speaker. When the speaker is done with speaking, the audience may clap their hands together to mark appreciation of the message or both the message and the speaker. However, when the hands are spontaneously and violently clapped, then it is a message that the audience should stop because what they are doing is unethical or irritating. At home, one of your parents probably clapped their hands suddenly and violently to make you stop as well as draw attention to their presence, especially where you were playing loudly around the house. Teachers may use this technique to restore in the class, especially where students were unaware that the teacher is around.

Then there is interlocking of one hand against those of the other hands and folding them. The use of this gesture indicates that one is attentive but unease at the same time. During an interview, meeting, or during a class session, the audience is likely to interlock their fingers and fold them.

In a way, the interlocking of the fingers is supposed to offer some form of assurance to the affected person that he or she is safe. One is likely to also use this gesture when he or she is mentioned negatively.

Think of how you reacted when you were mentioned among noisemakers or workers having challenges following the rules of the company. Most probably you interlocked your fingers and folded them.

When one is feeling shy or uncertain, the individual is also likely to interlock their fingers and raised the interlocked fingers when speaking. The gesture in this context appears to offer some sort of prop for the affected individual enabling them to navigate the anxiety. The gesture in this context is not just about communicating the physiological status of the affected person but as a coping mechanism of sudden anxiety and discomfort of the individual.

Another gesture involves raising both hands behind the head and interlocking the fingers to act as a cushion for the head. The gesture is used to indicate that one is feeling casual, tired, or simply not tasked by the current conversation. The gesture may also indicate that the individual is feeling tired by the conversation or the activity.

Think of how you react when feeling exhausted when talking to a friend or after watching a movie. You probably raised both of your hands, behind the head and interlocked the fingers to act as a headrest. In most cases, when one invokes this gesture, then the individual is likely to let the mind entertain other thoughts to escape from the current conversation.

Relatedly, there is the gesture where one lets one of their palms to brush down their faces. The gesture is used to signal deeper thinking, processing new contradictory information, or accepting humiliation in front of the audience. The gesture indicates surrender. It indicates yielding to inner thoughts or views from the audience that one may have initially opposed.

At one point, the class or your friends cornered a speaker facing the speaker to pause and take a minute to admit that he or she may have overlooked some facts about the issue. Probably the speaker used this gesture to indicate surrender.

For the audience and where the audience is seated continuously tapping on one's thighs with each individual finger-like playing the piano indicates that one is processing the message and that he or she is affected by the message at a personal level.

For instance, when you talk about police brutality and one of the audience members plays their fingers on their thighs like the way one plays the keys of a piano then the individual is feeling intense emotion listening to the message. It is a gesture and a way for the individual to safely process the intense emotion without experiencing an emotional outburst.

To indicate rejection or strong disagreement, both hands with palms wide are waved in an alternating manner to create letter X. In class, you probably drew the letter X using both hands to indicate that you disagree or reject what is being proposed. For instance, as a kid or as a student, you probably drew letter X to signal rejection that you will not follow instructions when the teacher sarcastically indicated that you should not follow his instructions.

On the other hand, when hands are open with palms down, then one is communicating that he or she is certain about what they are speaking. If your palms are facing each other with the fingers together, then you are communicating that you possess the expertise about what you are talking about. Then there is the approximation gesture which is carried out by holding out your hand horizontally, palm facing downward and with fingers forward, then tilting one's hand to the right and then left. The approximation gesture indicates that a statement is to be taken as an approximation.

Furthermore, moving with a gentle rocking in a left to right pattern is taken to be understood that it is not so good or not so bad. The gesture can be used to signal the other person when a match is going, and the friends are watching in the house, and they do not want to wake up the child through loud talking.

Additionally, there is the beckoning sign which has one's index finger sticking out of a fist and palm facing the gesturer. Then the finger moves constantly towards the interlocutor as to invite something closer. The beckoning sign has the general intent of commanding someone to where you are standing.

The beckoning sign is often performed with their four fingers using the whole hand depending on the distance of the recipient of the gesture is. Depending on the circumstance, when done with the index finger, it can have a potential sexual connotation. As a non-verbal communication, this gesture conveys the message of "come on" and "bring it." It can also be used as a taunt.

When one feels that the speaker is not making sense, he or she is likely to keep fingers straight and together while holding them upwards with the thumb pointing downwards. Then the thumb and fingers come together to indicate a talking mouth. The gesture is used to show contempt for an individual who is talking excessively about a topic that the interlocutor feels is trivial. In Asian cultures, the gesture is used as a reaction to a dry joke.

There is also the bunny ear, which is a joke and is widely used among children. The bunny ear consists of pointing up the index and middle finger akin to the "victory" sign and putting them behind the head to make it look a person has bunny ears. As a prank, it's commonly done when a picture is taken. The gesture may be appropriate during casual contexts.

Equally important is a clenched fist which is used across cultures to indicate defiance among a number of groups. The clenched fist is considered hostile and without any notionally offensive connotations. The clenched fist is associated with Communists and other nationalist revolutionary movements. In the United States, the clenched fist is associated with civil rights movements of the 1960s.

For the finger snap gesture, it is used to express that one is cornered. The gesturer usually holds a hand out in the adversary's direction and snaps their middle finger and thumb followed by facial expression and crossed arms. In the United Kingdom, snapping your fingers is used to indicate remembering or failing to do so. Kids may also snap their fingers to indicate that they are willing to answer.

In some contexts, the guns up gesture are used as a greeting or as a sign of victory during sporting events. The guns up gesture are done by placing the index finger forward and thumb upward. As such, the use of this gesture is high contextual even in the United States, where it is commonly used.

There is the hanging gesture that is realized by taking a closed fist at the side one's head and tilting it away from one's fist and performing a choking sound. The hanging gesture might also be accompanied by hanging out one's tongue loosely out the mouth and the rolling the eyes. The hanging gesture is used to indicate the interlocutor would rather be doing, and it could also be used to show suicide. The hanging gesture is increasingly being substituted by actual replication of a gun being shot at one's head.

Then there is the horn gesture which varies depending on the context. The horn gesture commonly denotes the horned god by neopagans. It is thought to ward off or to bestow the evil eye. In some places, the horn signs indicate a sexual innuendo or charging a man with being cheated on. It is used as an acknowledgement by fans of rock music usually with a repeated forward inclination of the wrist. When done in the context of music, it is known as the devil horns.

Aside from their critical role in communication, gestures help animate a conversation and add to the memorability of a conversion experience. You probably remember your teacher, coach, and preacher's message largely because it was accompanied by well-articulated gestures. Children and lovers may find gestures fun and also a validation of verbal communication. In this manner, gestures are essential for healthy parenting and for an improved relationship between lovers.

Chapter 7:

Posture and Body Orientation

Expectedly, posture, and body orientation should be interpreted in the context of the entire body language to develop the full meaning being communicated. Starting with an open posture, it is used to denote amicability and positiveness.

In this open position, the feet are placed openly, and the palms of the hands are facing outward. Individuals with open posture are deemed more persuasive compared to those with other stances.

To realize an open stance, one should stand upright or sit straight with the head upright and maintain the abdomen and chest bared. When the open posture is combined with an easy facial expression and good visual contact, it makes one look approachable and composed. Maintain the body facing forward toward the other person during a conversation.

There is also the closed posture where one crosses the arms across the chest or crosses the legs or sits in a facing a forward position as well as displaying the backs of the hands and closing the fists are indicative of a closed stance.

The closed posture gives the impression that one is bored, hostile, or detached. In this posture, one is acting cautious and appears ready to defend themselves against any accusation or threat.

For the confident posture, it helps communicate that one is not feeling anxious, nervous, or stressed. The confident posture is attained by pulling oneself to full height, holding the head high, and keeping the gaze at eye level. Then bring your shoulders backward and keep the arms as well as legs to relax by the sides. The posture is likely to be used by speakers in a formal context such as when making a presentation, during cross-examination and during project presentation.

Equally important, there is postural echoing and is used as a flirting technique by attracting someone in the Guardian. It is attained by observing and mimicking the style of the person and the pace of movement. When the individual leans against the wall, replicate the same.

By adjusting your postures against the others to attain a match, you are communicating that you are trying to flirt with the individual. The postural echoing can also be used as a prank game to someone you are familiar with and often engage in casual talk.

Maintaining a straight posture communicates confidence and formality. Part of the confidence of this posture is that it maximizes blood flow and exerts less pressure on the muscle and joints, which enhances the composure of an individual. The straight posture helps evoke desirable mood and emotion, which makes an individual feel energized and alert. A straight posture is highly preferred informal conversations such as during meetings, presentation, or when giving a speech.

Correspondingly being in a slumped position and hunched back is a poor posture and makes one be seen as lazy, sad, or poor. A slumped position implies a strain to the body, which makes the individual feel less alert and casual about the ongoing conversation.

On the other hand, leaning forward and maintaining eye contact suggests that one is listening keenly. During a speech, if the audience leans forward in an upright position, then it indicates that they are eager and receptive to the message.

Furthermore, if one slants one of the shoulders when participating in a conversation, then it suggests that the individual is tired or unwell. Leaning on one side acutely while standing or sitting indicates that you are feeling exhausted or fed up with the conversation and are eagerly waiting for the end or for a break.

Think of how you or others reacted when a class dragged on to almost break time. There is a high likelihood that the audience slanted one of their shoulders to left or right direction. In this state, the mind of the individual deviates to things that one will do next. In case of a tea break, the mind of the students will deviate to what one will do during or after the tea break.

By the same measure standing on one foot indicates that one is feeling unease or tired. When one stands on one foot, then it suggests that the person is trying to cope with uncomforting. The source of uneasiness could be emotional or physiological.

For instance, you probably juggled your body from one foot to help ease the need to go for a short call or pass wind. In most cases, one finds himself or herself standing on one foot when an uncomfortable issue is mentioned. It is a way to disrupt the sustained concentration that may enhance the disturbing feeling.

If one cups their head or face with their hands and rests the head on the thighs, then the individual is feeling ashamed or exhausted.

When the speaker mentions something that makes you feel embarrassed, then one is likely to cup their face or head and rest the face on the thighs. It is a literal way of hiding from shame.

Children are likely to manifest this posture though while standing. When standing this posture may make one look like he or she is praying.

Additionally, if one holds their arms akimbo while standing, then the individual is showing a negative attitude or disapproval of the message. The posture is created by holding the waist with both hands while standing up straight and facing the target person. The hands should simultaneously grip on the flanks, the part near the kidneys. In most cases, the arms-akimbo posture is accompanied by disapproval or sarcastic face to denote attitude, disdain, or disapproval.

When one stretches both of their shoulders and arms and rests them on chairs on either side, then the individual is feeling tired and casual. The posture is akin to a static flap of wings where one stretches their shoulder and arms like wings and rests them on chairs on either side. It is one of the postures that loudly communicates that you are bored, feeling casual, and that you are not about the consequences of your action.

The posture is also invasive of the privacy and space of other individuals and may disrupt their concentration.

If one bends while touching both of their knees, then the individual is feeling exhausted and less formal with the audience. The posture may also indicate extreme exhaustion and need to rest.

For instance, most soccer players bend without kneeling while holding both of their knees, indicating exhaustion. Since in this posture, one is facing down, the posture may be highly inappropriate in formal contexts and may make one appear queer.

When one leans their head and supports it with an open palm on the cheeks, then it indicates that one is thinking deep and probably feeling sad, sorrowful or depressed.

The posture is also used when one is watching something with a high probability of negative outcomes such as a movie or a game. The posture helps one focus deep on the issue akin to meditating.

Additionally, crossing your arms to touch shoulders or touch the biceps indicates that one is deliberately trying to focus on the issue being discussed. Through this posture, an individual tries to avoid distractions and think deeper on what is being presented.

If you watch European soccer, you will realize that coaches use this posture when trying to study the match, especially where their team is down. However, this posture should not be used in formal contexts as it suggests rudeness. The posture should be used among peers only.

Then there is the crossing of the legs from the thigh through the knee while seated on a chair, especially on a reclining chair. In this posture, one is communicating that he or she is feeling relaxed and less formal.

In most cases, this posture is exhibited when one is at home watching a movie or in the office alone past working hours. If this posture is replicated in a formal context, then it suggests boredom or lack of concentration.

For the posture where one crosses the legs from the ankle to the soles of the feet while seated, it communicates that one is trying to focus in an informal context such as at home. For instance, if a wife or a child asks the father about something that he has to think through, then the individual is likely to exhibit this posture. If this posture is replicated in a formal context, then it suggests boredom or lack of concentration.

Activity

a. Richard is attending a meeting on security, and the role that employees play in helping maintains the organization secure. During the first ten minutes of this meeting, Richard is seated upright with the head slightly leaning forward. Comment on what this implies.

b. Thirty minutes later, Richard slumps or slants in the chair while raising his head up and backward. Comment on what this means.

c. Forty-five minutes later, Richard has slanted his left shoulder and is supporting his head with the left hand while watching the speaker. Comment on what this implies.

d. After a twenty-minutes break, Richard sits upright with his arms crossed and palms touching the biceps. Comment on what this means.

e. After fifteen minutes, Richard stretches both of his arms across the top edges of the adjacent chairs while listening. Comment on this posture.

f. After twenty minutes, Richard crosses his legs from the thighs through the knees while listening. Comment on what this implies.

Chapter 8:
Voice

In line with other topics, voice as a form of non-verbal communication should be analyzed against other types of body language to reach a convincing conclusion. Individuals that work in customer care or call centers understand the value of voice. It is what the customer meets and forms an opinion of the service and the company. With respect to voice, what counts most is what one hears. A fan of music, you probably have comprehensive exposure to the role of voice in communication.

Starting with pitch, a high pitch indicates nervousness, and one should pitch inflection to convey energy and sound persuasive. Pitch concerns how loud a voice is when one is speaking. At one point, you might have felt unease having to shout on the phone due to the mouthpiece or network issues because it makes you sound nervous, and that is not how you want to be perceived. Listening to an individual that appears to be shouting suggests that the individual is irritated, tired, or unwell. A speaker that sounds like he or she is shouting comes across like someone that is offended or irked by an issue or the audience.

Then there is tone, which is critical because it can mislead or enhance the outcome of the conversation. If one has an angry tone, then it does not matter the neutrality of the message as the receiver will assume that the speaker is upset. A professional and understanding tone is preferred. A critical tone makes the person sound as if he or she is judging the audience. A professional tone makes one appear diplomatic and knowledgeable in what he or she is presenting to the audience.

Equally important is the speed of speaking. Speaking fast indicates panic and selfishness. Slowing down the speed of speaking allows the receiver to effectively process what is being spoken. Speaking fast also indicates that one is in a hurry and wants to move on to the next. If you have ever called a call center and got an agent that spoke fast than usual, then you felt the agent was listening or that the agent was not valuing your concern as it should be.

Correspondingly, try watching Sheldon Palmer in the TV series "The Big Bang Theory" and note the rate at which he speaks. While ignoring the personality of Sheldon Palmer in the TV series and focusing on the rate of speaking, why do you feel that Sheldon does not give the other person adequate time to express themselves? Do you think that the rate of speaking by Sheldon affects the intended message?

In detail, pitch concerns the lowness or highness of the voice and is highly critical in the English language. Through pitch, we express emotions and attitudes by changing intonation. From the pitch of the voice, we can determine if one is feeling stressed. Variation of pitch helps make the conversation sound natural as emotions are not static. From the analysis of pitch variation, one can determine if one is a native or non-native speaker of a language. A monotone voice is not expressive and not interesting to hear.

It is important to acknowledge that tone also includes verbal communication, especially the choice of words. The kind of words that one employs affects the intended tone despite the best intention of the individual. However, in this context, we are focusing on non-verbal communication.

At one point, you tried making a joke, but no one laughed, or you had to offer apologies because the audience processed differently. Part of this mishap was due to the way you voiced the joke making it appear like shouting, taunting or disdain. Even the best comedians lose the audience in some instances due to the way they voiced their joke.

As indicated, having a consistent content tone of voice enables the audience to view you as consistent. At school or campus, you profiled and expected your teachers or dons to speak in a speaking manner. Part of this profiling is attributed to the consistency of their voice's tone.

Take time and search the late and former United Nations secretary general Koffi Annan to appreciate the pitch and voice of a speaker. There is a justification for insisting on tone during communication.

Notably, the role of tone in communication is to make you appear human. People prefer to deal with humans, and tone helps develop a relatable personality that the customer can bond with. The rising and falling of tone help make the communication natural, and the recipient of the message views the communication as not rehearsed. Having the same tone will make one sound monotonous as well as appear rehearsed.

If you sound monotonic, then it is suggesting that you cannot elicit the emotional aspects of the communication, and this makes you appear less human to the audience. Most probably, one of your favorite actors effectively uses tone to convey different emotions. At the national level, your favorite political figure varies the tone making the message appear live and relatable.

Having a distinctive tone can help woo and convince your customers. It is not just about having a pleasant tone but also about identity. If one shows a consistent and particular tone, then the public is likely to form an image of your values and personality, and this can make it easier to connect with customers. For instance, your favorite social media influencer has a particular tone that you associate the individual with and have learned to find it a unique way to approach issues.

Additionally, tone replaces face to face communication, and this makes tone highly critical to avoid misconceptions and backlash. As earlier on indicated, as most services go online, most customers occasionally need assistance with applications and access to online services, and this requires an effective call center.

When customers contact the call center, the only thing they interact with is the tone of the speaker. The tone of the call agent can exacerbate the emotions of the client or thaw their emotions and make it easier to solve the issue facing the customer.

Furthermore, the tone helps build authority. You most probably know someone who sounds commanding, authoritative, and uncertain courtesy of tone of the person.

A consistent and natural tone suggests confidence in what one is speaking about, and this makes the person appear in charge. Try watching National Geographic wildlife documentaries or Ted Freedoms, and you will realize that the narrators and speakers have a consistent and natural varying tone to suggest confidence in what they are talking about.

Through tone, one sustains the focus of the communication. Expectedly, tone helps keep the audience positioned in what the speaker intended. For instance, a professional tone helps maintain communication as formal. Again using the call center example, most call agents politely try to keep the conversation formal even when the caller tries deviating the communication. The tone of the conversation makes the audience appreciate the formality level of the conversation.

Finally, tone helps one develop an identity. As indicated, you regard certain people as commanding, comical, or reserved based on their tone, among other factors. Again, try recalling which celebrity or politician sounds convincing, professional, commanding, or angry. The tone is connected to the way people feel the emotion you are trying to communicate. In some cases, the tone contradicts the intended emotion distorting the emotion.

Activity

a. How do you feel standing or sitting next to someone that is shouting on the phone even though the person is speaking about pleasant news? Have you ever been in a place that is out of network coverage and you had to shout? How did you feel if your response to the previous question is yes?

b. Do you know of an individual that sounds judgmental or sarcastic even though that is not the intention of the person? For instance, do you know about an individual that is wrongly perceived as rude or uncaring because of the way the person talks even though the individual is caring and respectful, but the voice gives away the person?

c. In a pair or three people, try giving a speech with a flat tone, vary the tone in the second episode, in the third episode try to sound judgmental and in the last episode try to sound commanding. If alone, you can record yourself and listen to the recordings later. Then have a friend to listen and judge each of the episode, which episode did your friend find natural and comfortable to listen to?

d. Finally, search YouTube for industrial strikes in the United Kingdom and the United States and listen to the pitch and tone of the leaders. Now search for industrial strikes in any African or Asian countries that speak English and listen to the pitch and tone of the leaders.

Then comment on the tone variation or lack of tone variation in the selected leaders of the industrial leaders. Go further and comment on the pitch of the selected leaders of the industrial strikes. Then listen to any speech by Barack Obama and a speech by Teresa May. Which of the two sounds convincing and natural to listen to?

Chapter 9:
Space and Distance

Using the context of the United States, there are four kinds of distances that people use to interact on a face-to-face basis. These distances are intimate, personal, social, and public distances. Starting with intimate distance, it is utilized for highly secretive exchanges as this zone is marked by zero to two feet of separation between two folks. An form of intimate distance includes two individuals hugging, standing next to each other, or holding hands. Individuals' intimate distance have a common unique level of familiarity with one another. If one is not comfortable with a person approaching them in their intimate proximity will experience a significant amount of situational discomfort.

Correspondingly, personal space is used for communicating with relatives as well as close acquaintances. Even though this grants an individual a bit more space compared to the intimate space, it is still relative proximity of that intimate space and may involve touching. The personal distance can have a breadth from two to four feet. Akin to intimate proximity, if an unknown person walks into the personal zone, the one is likely to feel uneasy being in such close quarters with a stranger.

Furthermore, there is the social distance that used in professional exchanges or when meeting folks while interrelating with groups. Compared to the other distances, social distance has a larger scope in the range that it can accommodate. Its scope is four to twelve feet, and it depends on the context. It is used among students, acquaintances, or co-workers. As expected, most participants in the social distance do not show physical interaction among themselves. Generally, people are likely to be very specific concerning the degree of social distance that is preferred as some require more physical distance compared to others. In most cases, the individual will adjust backward or forward to get the appropriate social distance necessary for social interactions.

By the same measure, we have public distance, which is twelve or more feet between folks. A good measure of public distance is where two individuals sit on a bench in a public park. In most cases, the two people on a bench in a public park will sit at the farthest ends from each other to preserve the public space. Each of the earlier types of proximity will significantly impact an individual's perception of what is the appropriate type of distance in specific contexts. One of the factors that contribute to individual perceptions of how proxemics should be used is culture. Individuals from different cultures show different viewpoints on what the appropriate persona; space should be.

Additionally, there is the concept of territoriality, where individuals tend to feel like they own and should control their personal areas. When someone invades this personal space, then the individual will react negatively as it is an invasion of territory without express permission. At one point, you asked a stranger to keep some distance from you because you felt uncomfortable with the person standing close to you. Sometimes standing next to a person may also denote that you are creepy and may be intending to harm the person.

When talking to someone and the individual invades your personal space, and you allow it then it signals that you are okay to intimate ideas. Intimate ideas in this context include highly personal issues that one can talk with another person. For instance, if you walk and sit close and in contact with a lady watching television and she approves your behavior, then it is indicative that she is likely to allow you have a personal talk that may be intimate in nature. Such talk may include your health challenges or mental health and not necessarily sexual issues. For this reason, one should carefully weigh the need to invade the personal distance.

For the case of children, invading personal distance will make them freeze due to feeling uncomfortable. If a teacher sits next to a student or stands next to a student, then the student is likely to feel uneasy and nervous. However, they are instances where the invasion of personal space is allowed and seen as necessary. For instance, during interviews or when being examined by a doctor, invasion of private space by the person with leverage is allowed. The panel during an interview may move or ask you to move closer, which may violate your personal space. A doctor may also stand closer to you, invading your personal space, but this is necessary due to the professional demand of their service.

In the analysis, when one avoids personal distance, and the individual is expected to be within this space, then the individual may be feeling less confident or feeling ashamed. For instance, if a child has done something embarrassing, he or she is likely to sit or stand far from the parent during a conversation. For this reason, it appears that one should feel confident, assured, and appreciated to approach and remain in personal space when needed.

Sometimes staying in the personal space during intense emotions may portray one as resilient, understanding, and bold. Think of two lovers or sibling quarreling, but each remains in the established personal space. The message that is being communicated is that the individual is confident that he or she can handle the intense emotions from the other person. Since being in personal space places a person within physical striking range, most people will only allow trusted and familiar individuals into their personal space.

In some instances, invasion of personal space is justified because it is part of professional demands. Think of a new teacher that is trying to help a student solve a mathematical equation. In this aspect, the teacher is a stranger because he or she is new to the school. By sitting or standing close to the student, the teacher is invading the personal space, but the established norms in this context allow the student not to feel unease. For emphasis, this case is not unique as it aligns with stated expectations that people will welcome known or unfamiliar people in their personal space only if they trust them and in this case, the student feels safe with any teacher. For this reason, the operationalization of distance in communication is mediated and moderated by established culture.

In reality, one can start with public distance before allowing the interaction to happen in personal or social space. For instance, as a student during tournaments, you could have initiated non-verbal communication with the student from the other college before suddenly feeling connected to the individual and allowing him or her to move into personal space as a potential girlfriend or boyfriend.

At first, the target person saw you as a stranger but allowed you to make non-verbal communication within the public space. When the person felt the need to connect more with you and have given you a benefit of doubt, the person allowed you to move through public distance and social distance to enter their personal space.

A lot can be learned from studying distance and space in communication. Being allowed into the social and personal distances implies that the person trusts that you will not harm them emotionally and physically. For the intimate distance, being allowed into this distance implies that the person trusts you so much and is confident that you can never harm them and that you share a lot.

For instance, a mother holding her baby close enough to her signals that the baby is feeling assured of security and protection. When two lovers move closer till their faces are almost touching, it suggests trust and confidence that the other person feels safe and protected.

On the other hand, if arguing with your child or lover and the individual moves farther from you physically, then it suggests that the person no longer feels safe with you being within their personal distance. Issues that can cause someone to expand the distance between you and them include the risk of violence from you and emotional issues.

If you occasionally act violent, then chances are that your lover or children will expand the personal distance to social distance because this is where they feel safe due to your personality and character.

However, they are other issues that cause individuals to extend the distance of interaction, and these include having a medical condition or having hygiene issues. For instance, if you are sweaty, then chances are that the other person may prefer to extend the distance of communication between you and them.

Having oral hygiene issues may also make the other person move far away from you because the smell turns them off. Having some medical conditions can make people maintain some distance from you or be closer to you physically. For instance, some conditions may attract uneasiness, and this includes epilepsy. People with epilepsy get seizures, and this can make people feel unease being closer to them because they inadvertently fall.

On the other hand, having hearing issues or sore throat may make people move closer to you physically to facilitate effective communication. However, these are exceptions when analyzing space and distance as forms of non-verbal communication, but they should be taken into account where necessary.

Some contexts allow for the invasion of personal distance merely by circumstances. For instance, when attending a match in a full packed stadium or sitting to watch a movie in a movie theater, one will have his personal invaded due to the sitting arrangements.

In this context, one may feel unease with this arrangement, but he or she has little control of the situation. While we value and seek to protect personal spaces, there are situations that make us allowing invasion of this space because it is beyond control.

Activity

a. Richard is talking to his girlfriend, and their noses are almost touching. Comment on what this means.

b. The following day, Richard is talking to his girlfriend while standing 9 feet away. Comment on what this means.

c. An elderly person asks Richard to assist him in how to shop online using the smartphone. Richard is standing right next to this elderly person. Comment on what this means.

d. On Saturday, Richard had an argument with his sister, he was visibly angry, but they continued exchanging words while seated on the same sofa set. Comment on this distance and space in communication. Comment on the importance of trust and assurance for people who share this space.

e. Richard met his girlfriend while attending a football match. It all started when Richard through a hard stare at her at the farthest end of the stand. When the girl reciprocated the stare, Richard moved closer to her after the game and they walked holding hands. This is an example of allowing someone to transit from public distance to personal distance.

Using analysis of distance and space in communication only, why do you think the girl allowed Richard to shorten the distance and welcome him into the personal space?

f. Mitchell works as a nurse at the local clinic. When one of the patients asked for a nurse, Mitchell moved close enough to the patient and touched his hand to examine it. What is the justification for this distance in this communication?

g. Mitchell and her husband had a quarrel last night, and today they sat eight feet from each other while pretending nothing happened. Using the concept of space and distance only, suggest two reasons for this behavior?

h. As a new mother, Mitchell holds her baby closer, making her nose and that of the baby touch while making sounds to the baby. Justify why this distance and space in communication is allowed?

i. Last month while seated on a bench in a public park, a stranger walked and sat right next to Mitchell even though the bench had only Mitchell. Mitchell decided to stand up and walk away. Why do you think Mitchell walked away? Use only the concept of distance and space to explain.

Chapter 10:
Touch

We engage in touching routinely, and it includes patting someone or giving someone a hug to indicate our concern and appreciation. We commonly shake hands as greetings or assign to signal shared understanding. Touch, as a form of communication, is called haptics. For children, touch is a crucial aspect of their development.

Children that do not get adequate touch have developmental issues. Touch helps babies cope with stress. At infancy, touch is the first sense that a baby acknowledges.

Functional touch

At the workplace, touch is among effective means of communication, but it is necessary to follow common norms of etiquette. For instance, a handshake is a means of touching that is utilized in business settings and can convey the relationship between two people.

Pay attention to the non-verbal signals that you are transmitting next time you shake someone's hand. In overall, one should always convey confidence when shaking another person's hand, but you should avoid being overly-confident. Praise and encouragement are communicated by a tap on the back or a hand on a shoulder.

For instance, an innocent touch can make another person feel unease, and for this reason, applying touch requires reading the body language and responding accordingly.

A standard measure is that it is better to fail but on the side of caution. Functional touch includes being physically examined by a doctor and being touch as a form of professional massage.

Social touch

The majority of communication requires some kind of contact. A handshake is the main form of touch in social touches. Handshakes vary from culture to culture. It is socially accepted and allowed for one to shake another person's hand during a first meeting in the United States. In other cultures, a kiss on the cheek is perfectly acceptable.

In the same interactions, men will allow a male stranger to touch their shoulders and/or arms, whereas women may allow touch by a female stranger, but only on the arms and/or hands.

Men are likely to enjoy touch from a female while women tend to feel uncomfortable with any form of touching from a male. Equally important, males and females process touch distinctly, which may create confusing and potentially uncomfortable situations. In most contexts, it might help unneeded physical contact in social contexts, especially those of the opposite gender.

One should try to follow social norms and to take clues from those in your proximity. For instance, while you are standing next to a stranger in an elevator, its not appropriate to engage in any unnecessary physical touch with them.

Friendship touch

The types of physical contact allowed between friends vary depending on contexts. For instance, women are more receptive, touching female friends compared to their male counterparts.

The touches between female friends show more affectionate often in the form of hugging, whereas males prefer a handshake and/or a pat on the back. Within relatives, women tend to have more physical contact as compared to men. Additionally, same-sex family members tend to have more contact with relatives opposite gender.

Signs of affection among friends are critical in expressing encouragement and support, even if you are not a touchy person. One should be prepared to get out of one's comfort zone and offer their friend a warming gesture when they are going through a difficult time. Helping others enliven their moods is likely to uplift your moods as well.

Intimacy touch

In romantic relationships, touches that communicate love play a critical role. For instance, the simplest of touches can convey a critical meaning such as hand-holding or placing you're an arm around a partner, which communicates that they are a couple. Women place more premiums on touch compared to men, and even the smallest of gestures can help calm women they were upset.

Arousal touch

Arousing contact elicit intense feelings and are only suitable through mutual consent. Arousal touches are intended to evoke joy and pleasure and can involve kissing, flirtatious touching, hugging that is meant to suggest sexual interaction. One should be careful about their partner's needs. One can greatly improve their communication skills and relationships by paying attention to the non-verbal cues that you transmit via physical contact.

Additionally, our sense of touch is intended to communicate clearly and quickly. Touch can elicit subconscious communication. For instance, you instantly pull away from your hand when touching something hot even before you consciously process. In this manner, touch constitutes one of the quickest ways to communicate. Touch, as a form of non-verbal communication, is an instinctive form of communication. In detail, touch conveys information instantly and causes a guttural reaction. Completely withholding touch will communicate the wrong messages without your realization.

Ways of improving touch in appropriate contexts

Pat someone on the back when you grant them praise.

If your colleague or friend has graduated, earned a promotion or married, then pat them on the back. Giving a pat suggests that you are happy with the person and are encouraging them. Touch has a therapeutic value that relaxes the mind and the body as well as helping an individual feel secure and appreciated. At school, you must have felt valued and loved if you were patted on the back.

Initiate discussions with a touch to create cooperative relationships.

Studies have established that touching a person increases their willingness to cooperate and work with others.

Establishing physical contact with an individual that you wish to initiate a conversation with can help. Sometimes the target person may not realize that you touched them but will register subconsciously and establish a bond.

Extend the handshakes.

Shaking hands shows confidence and simplicity in interacting with others. Touch helps build trust between two people. Make your handshakes firm when shaking hands with people.

It is also necessary to remember that some health conditions may make one shy away from shaking hands, and this include hyperhidrosis, which makes the palms of the person sweat. With sweaty hands, the individual is likely to shun handshakes, and this has little to do with the context of the conversation.

Adjust the touch type with respect to context

As indicated, touch is highly contextual. For instance, the Japanese do not favor shaking hands, and a person in this environment will avoid shaking hands at all costs. In the American context, shaking hands is encouraged.

For this reason, one should adjust their touch type depending on the contexts. It might be welcome to hold the hands of your partner continuously while the same is creepy when talking to a stranger or to a colleague at the workplace.

Another form of touch is tickling, which is mostly reserved for lovers, parents versus children, and peers. For instance, a mother may tickle her baby, which is a therapeutic touch and is permissible. On the hand, children or students of the same age set may tickle each other, which are permissible. However, it is inappropriate to tickle an adult when you are not lovers or the relationship between you and them is formal.

Touch as a form of abuse

Expectedly, there is a thin line between permissible touch and physical abuse. If not certain one should avoid initiating touch unless fully certain of its meaning to the target person. Pushing someone or pinching someone is considered a form of physical abuse. Kicking or striking someone as well as strangling, are forms of physical abuse.

Touch as a game

In some contexts, a touch is a form of the game, especially teasing. Touch as a form of the game should only happen where the participants are peers and are receptive to it. For instance, your friend or classmate may blindfold your eyes with the palms of their hands from behind.

The participants in this tease may touch each other; for instance, the blinded person may try to feel your arms or head to try to guess the identity of the person teasing. In this form of touch, the scope of teaching allowed is large and may be equivalent to that of lovers.

Activity

a. Alex held the hand of a new employee, a lady, for more than three minutes while talking to her. Comment on this form of touch. Was it appropriate?

b. Nicole held the face of her child, wiping clean the face with the palm of her hands. Comment on this touch.

c. Brian went for professional massage and was comfortable with the masseuse. Why was Brian receptive to this form of touch?

d. You are seated on a bench in a public park when suddenly you notice a man trying hard to hug a lady that is resisting the attempt. The man then tries to land one of his arms on her thighs, and the lady walks away. Comment on the inappropriate touch in this context.

e. Jimmy was taking a walk in the park when he saw a child crying with the mother around. Jimmy introduced himself and invited the child to his arms. The child gladly allowed Jimmy to lift her and hold her. Comment on this type of touch. Why were both the child and the mother willing to let Jimmy touch the child?

f. Anastasia avoids shaking hands at her workplace even though she has no physical condition such as hyperhidrosis that can hinder handshakes. When Anastasia shakes your hands, the handshake is weak. Comment on this touch as her manager.

g. Yvonne was shedding tears after failing to appear on the pass list at her college. John, who was standing next to her, gave her a warm and reassuring hug which Yvonne did not want to let go. Why was this form of touch therapeutic to Yvonne in this context?

Chapter 11:
Paralinguistic

A type of non-verbal communication that is premised on the qualities of voice and the manner one vocalizes them is known as paralinguistic. The accent, pitch, and tone of our voice communicate more about us and our personality. Our accent can tell where we come from or our teachers.

The audience will, for instance, form stereotypes based on your accent. An individual that talks slow may sound tired, thoughtful, or perhaps not intelligent. An individual that talks fast may sound shady, anxious, or excited. Inflection, vocal volume, and stammering do influence verbal messages and affect the processing of the intended meaning by the audience.

In this manner, paralinguistic entails the aspects of spoken communication that does not involve words. For this reason, paralinguistic emphasize or diminish the intended meaning of what people say. Other aspects of body language are part of paralinguistic.

The features of language that are paralinguistic are critical as they directly influence the message. Better conversation can be realized by being more aware of the subtle nuances of verbal communication by promoting deeper understanding and connection with others. In overall, the study of voice and how words are voiced is paralinguistic communication.

Speed or rate of speaking

Speaking faster or rapid rates of speech are linked to composure and self-assurance. One should try to speak at a rate similar to the individual they are communicating with in conversation. In the TV series "Young & Hungry" watch a single episode and focus on Gabi Diamond. In the TV series, Gabi Diamond speaks fast, and this makes her look like she is exhibiting composure and self-assurance.

However, if you watch several episodes, you will realize that she speaks fast to hide her insecurities and disappointments with love largely due to her quick nature of approaching love issues. Against this backdrop, speaking rapidly may suggest composure and self-assurance, but it is not necessarily the true status of the individual.

Think of a classmate or colleague that speaks fast. Chances are that the individual has composure and self-assurance or the person is masking their insecurities. People that naturally speak fast are the ones that may be exhibiting composure and self-confidence. However, individually that suddenly speaks fast than usual may be showing attempts to hide their weakness.

In public speaking, an individual may speak fast, try to showcase all before the expiry of the indicated time. In overall, the assessment of the rate of speaking should largely be naturally fast speaker versus induced fast speaking. Speaking fast for an individual that does not speak at that rate may be indicative of attempts to trivialize the situation or create lies.

Rhythm

Most languages exhibit unique rhythms, and rhythm is critical, especially for the English language. A person from Singapore and one from France will speak at a different speed and rhythm. In most cases, people will speak a second language at a rhythmical pace similar to their native language.

The overall aim of acknowledging rhythm is that you should try to speak at the same rhythm with the individual, and the chosen rhythm should be the one that is slower than the other. At one point, you tried having a conversation with a person that is not a native speaker of English, and you had to slow down the conversation to enhance understanding.

To appreciate the criticality of rhythm, search YouTube for "Kids stories English India" and note the rhythm of Indian speakers of English. You will realize that the speakers try to speak close to the rhythm of their native language. Again, go to YouTube and search for "President's speech Uganda, Kenya, Nigeria or Zambia." You will observe that the speaking rhythm is close to the native language rhythm of the speaker.

As suggested, the person with fast rhythm has to adjust to the slower rhythm. Search YouTube for "BBC interview with Uganda's president Museveni" or "CNN interview with Kenya's President Kenyatta." In any instances of these interviews, you will realize that the interview tries to slow their usual rhythm of speaking to match the relatively slow rhythm of these African countries' presidents. On the contrary, if you voice the person with the slow rhythm to match up to your fast pace, then the conversation will negatively be affected as the individual will have to rush their thoughts and reactions.

Volume

Speaking loud suggests that one is assertive, confident, and bold. Think of a politician or any leader that you recognize. Chances are that the individual speaks loud enough, which shows that the person is confident and assured of what he or she is saying. When addressing the entire school, your college principle spoke with loud volume, which indicated authority and certainty of what he or she was saying.

On the other hand, speaking with low volume shows shyness and insecurity. For instance, in school, the groups that had not done adequate preparation during presentation probably spoke with low volume. The ones that had researched and fine-tuned their work spoke confidently. If you are a parent, you will notice that if your child has done something awkward, then he or she will reply in low voice almost muffled voice.

Pitch

Speaking with a high-pitched voice makes one sound childlike. Lower pitches are largely associated with higher credibility, authority, and maturity. Try listening to Bernadette Rostenkowski, the character wife to Howard Wolowitz in the TV series "The Big Bang Theory." She features from season 6 onwards.

Take note of Bernadette Rostenkowski pitch in the TV series. The most important thing is that the pitch you choose should be your most powerful vocal range. You should not force a lower pitched voice even if it is considered more credible as you risk losing the vocal power.

For emphasis, speaking in low-pitched voice indicates that you have owned the space and are confident in what you are expressing. Most people find people with deep voices as appealing to listen to and hold a conversation with. Men have an advantage when it comes to low-pitch voices, and this easily makes them come across as composed and in charge. The low pitch voice is a critical element of talk therapy as it gives reassurance and calming effect to the target person.

Inflection

Vocal variety or inflection concerns the variations in the pitch of the voice. Some contexts demand variations in pitch such as when narrating a story to children while other contexts demand less variation in pitch, such as in the corporate world. A few singing exercises when showering can help improve tone variation of the voice. The other great way to practice is to record and listen to oneself to analyze the quality of your inflection.

When listening to someone, pay attention to inflection. A person that shows expected tonal variation of the voice is speaking naturally and probably is truthful. People that speak a monotone are likely disinterested or not being truthful. However, some instances may justify speaking with no tonal variation in casual contexts. For instance, people that are not native speakers of English are likely to speak with a flat tone and this because they lack the native perception of the choice of the words used. Additionally, for most people, when reading a text are likely to use a flat tone as opposed to speaking their minds literally.

Equally important, some cultures and languages favor variation of tone. For instance, American English and Lingala language are widely spoken in the Democratic Republic of Congo naturally demands tonal variation of the voice. The phonetics of these languages give the speakers the quality of varying tone compared to say the Swahili language widely spoken in East Africa.

In this manner, the cultural context of the language may enhance or lower the degree of inflection when one is speaking. Lastly, a tonal variation of the voice does not imply shouting as one can speak softly but vary the tone.

Quality

The attribute of voice that enables you to distinguish one voice from another is known as the quality of the voice. For instance, identifying a voice as feminine or aloof constitutes the quality of the voice. Quality of a voice is a function of pitch, rate, and volume of voice. Even though the quality of voice can be learned, in most cases, it is innate. Some people are born with a commanding voice or feminine voice.

The quality of voice is largely monetized when one decides to work as a musician, narrator or news anchor. Despite having different voice qualities, some contexts seek and use different voice qualities, especially in animation movies and general movies where the different quality of voices are critical to eliciting laughter and relatable aspects of the production.

Perhaps the best illustration of different voice qualities is the TV animation series, "Family Guy." Search for an episode of "Family Guy" and notice the different voice qualities. Before you search, kindly appreciate that some of the content may sound offensive to people with disabilities, and ethnic minorities.

However, most of the content is standard with a touch of humor. Listen to the quality of voice of the character Louis and that of the character Peter Griffin. Again, listen to the quality of voice of Joe and that of Stewie, all characters. You can also look for any animation, and I suggest "The Storks" and "Penguins of Madagascar" to appreciate the quality of voice. Most animation movies present different voice qualities within a short period of time, enabling you to register and analyze them.

Tone

With respect to voice, tone regards the intensity of the voice. The tone of a voice reveals more about the emotions behind the words being spoken.

If the listener is assertive, then he or she will quickly connect and create a rapport with someone on the telephone by utilizing aspects of paralinguistic communication. Creating a rapport can be enhanced through matching and mirroring vocal attributes devoid of mockery.

All these lead to greater understanding and more effective paralinguistic communication. Realizing awareness of your paralinguistic vocal strengths will enable one to subtly influence the speaking and listening so that one comes across as a powerful communicator.

Equally important is that the loudness of a voice varies across cultures. For instance, men in Saudi Arabia may sound aggressive when compared against the loudness of voice in the United States. Among Arabs, a soft tone implies weakness. Personal social class also impacts the loudness of voice with people in lower classes using lower volumes when speaking. The tone of the voice is what feels that someone is angry.

For non-Americans outside America, they may struggle to notice the sarcasm in the laughter of some Americans. Americans tend to apply sarcasm in speech and laughter that non-Americans may miss unless they understand tone. When speaking or interacting with a non-American one should understand that the person may not get the sarcasm, and this may impede effective conversation. In overall, when using tonal variation to elicit sarcasm, one should be careful with respect to the ethnic and nationality composition of the audience.

Chapter 12:
How to Instantly Read People

Reading people is not entirely the forte of psychiatrist even though psychiatrists are best placed to read people. Reading people requires deciphering their verbal and non-verbal cues. When reading people, you should try to remain objective and open to new information.

Nearly each one of us has some form of personal bias and stereotypes that blocks our ability to correctly understand another person. When reading an individual, it is necessary to reconcile that information against the profession and cultural demands on the target person.

How to detect specific personality traits

As indicated earlier on, body language provides the most authoritative emotional and physiological status of an individual. It is difficult to fake all forms of non-verbal communication, and this makes body language critical in understanding a person.

Verbal communication can be faked through rehearsal and experience, and this can give misleading stance. When analyzing people, analyze the different types of communications skills as a set.

For instance, analyze facial expressions, body posture, pitch, tonal variation, touch and eye contact as a related but different manifestation of communication and emotional status. For instance, when tired, one is likely to stretch their arms and rest them on the left and right tops of adjacent chairs, sit in a slumped position, stare at the ceiling and drop their heads.

Analyzing only one aspect of body language can mislead one in the conclusion. Where verbal communication and non-verbal communication conflict, one should prioritize non-verbal communication.

Next, you should pay attention to appearance. The first impression counts, but it can also be misleading. In professional contexts, the appearance of an individual is critical to communicate the professionalism of the person and the organizational state of the mind of that individual.

For instance, an individual with an unbuttoned shirt indicates he hurried or is casual with the audience and the message. Donning formal attire that is buttoned and tucked in suggests prior preparation and seriousness that the person lends to the occasion. Having unkempt hair may indicate a rebellious mind, and this might be common among African professors in Africa.

In most contexts, having unkempt hair suggests that one lacks the discipline to prepare for the formal context or the person is overworked and is busy. Lack of expected grooming may suggest an individual battling with life challenges or feeling uncared for.

Equally important one should take note of the posture of the person. As discussed earlier, posture communicates a lot about the involvement of an individual in a conversation. Having an upright posture suggests eagerness and active participation in what is being communicated.

Cupping one's face in the arms and letting the face rest on both thighs suggests that one is feeling exhausted or has deviated from the conversation completely. Having crossed arms suggests defensiveness or deep thought. Sitting in a slumped position suggests that one is tired and not participating in the ongoing conversation. Leaning on the wall or any object suggests casualness that the person is lending to an ongoing conversation.

At home, sitting with crossed legs suggests that one is completely relaxed. However, the same posture at the workplace indicates that one is feeling tensed and at the same time concentrating.

Additionally, watch for physical movements in terms of distance and gestures. The distance between you and the person one is communicating communicates about the level of respect and assurance that the individual perceives.

A social distance is the safest bet when communicating, and it suggests high levels of professionalism or respect between the participants. Human beings tend to be territorial as exhibited by the manner that they guard their personal distance. Any invasion of the personal distance will make the individual defensive and unease with the interaction.

For this reason, when an individual shows discomfort when the distance between communicators is regarded as social or public, then the individual may have other issues bothering him or her. Social and public distances should make one feel fully comfortable. Allowing a person close enough or into the personal distance suggests that the individual feels secure and familiar with the other person. Reading the distance between the communicators will give a hint on the respect, security, and familiarity between the individuals as well the likely profession of the individuals.

Furthermore, the try to interpret facial expressions as deep frown lines indicate worry or over-thinking. Facial expressions are among the visible and critical forms of body language and tell more about the true emotional status of an individual. For instance, twitching the mouth suggests that an individual is not listening and is showing disdain to the speaker.

A frozen face shows that the individual is shell-shocked, and this can happen when making a presentation of health and diseases or when releasing results of an examination. A smiling face with the smile not being prolonged suggests that one is happy and following the conversation. A prolonged smile suggests sarcasm. Continually licking the lips may suggest that one is lying or that one is feeling disconnected from the conversation.

By the same measure, create a baseline for what qualifies as normal behavior. As you will realize that each person has distinct mannerisms that may be misleading to analyze them as part of the communication process. For instance, some individuals will start a conversation by looking down or at the wall before turning to the audience. In a mild way, mannerisms are like a ritual that one must activate before they make a delivery. Additionally, each person uniquely expresses the possible spectra of body language.

By establishing a baseline of what is normal behavior, one gets to accurately identify and analyze deviations from the standardized normal behavior. In this manner, one will not erratically judge a speaker that shuffles first if that is part of his behavior when speaking to an audience.

Additionally, pay attention to inconsistencies between the established baseline that you have created and the individual's gestures and words. Once you have created a baseline then scout for any deviations from this baseline. For instance, if one speaks in a high-pitched voice that is uncharacteristically of the individual, then the person may be feeling irritated.

If one normally walks across the stage when speaking but the individual during the current speech choose to speak from a fixed position then the person is exhibiting a deviation that may suggest that the individual is having self-awareness or is feeling unease with the current audience. If an individual speaks fast, but usually the person speaks with a natural flow, then the person is in a hurry or has not prepared for the task.

Based on this baseline which you have created about a person, or group, you can then detect any unusual or abnormal behavior. This can be a clue into potential deception, lying or any other signal that they are hiding something from you. In addition, this will allow you to become familiar with the way individuals may shift their ideas or priorities when it comes to their relationship with you.

As indicated, view gestures as clusters to elicit a meaning of what the person is communicating or trying to hide. During speaking a person will express different gestures and dwelling on current gesture may make you arrive at a misleading conclusion. Instead, one should view the gestures as clusters and make an interpretation of what they imply.

For instance, if a speaker throws the hands randomly in the air, raises one of their feet, stamps the floor and shakes the hands then all of these could suggest a speaker that is feeling irked and disappointed by the audience or the message. By the same measure, the different aspects of body language should be interpreted as a unit rather than in isolation.

Go further and compare and contrast. For one to fully read the target person, try comparing the body language of the person against the entire group or audience. For instance, if one appears bored and other people appear bored, then you should conclude the tiredness of the person is largely due to actions of the speaker for speaking longer than necessary. In other terms, the non-verbal cues of the target person is not isolated.

However, if you make a comparison, and it happens that the target person's bodily cues deviated from the rest, then you should profile the actions of the individual accordingly. Making a comparison and contrast helps make a fair judgment of the target person.

Similarly, try to make the person react to your deliberate communication. Another way of managing to read a person is to initiate communication and watch their reaction. For instance, establishing eye contact and evaluating the reciprocation of the target person can help tell more about their confidence and activeness in participating in the interaction. When an individual ignores your attempts to initiate communication, the person could be concentrating on other things, or the person feels insecure. Initiating communication is necessary where it is difficult to profile a person, and one wants to convincingly read the person.

Again try to identify the strong voice. A strong voice suggests the confidence and authority of the speaker. If the speaker lacks a strong voice, then he or she is new to what is being presented or has stage fright. However, having a strong voice that is not natural suggests a spirited attempt to appear in charge and confident. A strong voice should be natural if the individual is feeling composed and confident in what he or she is talking about.

Then observe how the individual walks. When speaking to a target person, he or she will walk across the stage or make movements around the site that the conversation is happening.

From the manner of walking, we can read a lot about the individual. Frequently walking up and down while speaking to an audience, may suggest panic or spirited attempt to appear in control. Speaking while walking slowly across the stage from one end to the other end indicates that one is comfortable speaking to the audience. If a member of the audience poses a question, and one walks towards the individual, then it suggests interest in clarifying what the individual is asking.

Try to scout for personality cues. Fortunately, all people have identifiable personalities, but these can be difficult to read for a person not trained in a psychologist. However, through observation, one will get cues on the personality of the individual. For instance, an outgoing person is likely to show a warm smile and laugh at jokes.

A socially warm person is likely to want to make personal connections when speaking, such as mentioning a particular person in the audience. Reserved people are likely to be laconic in their communication and appear scared or frozen on stage when speaking.

Equally important, one should listen to intuition as it is often valid. Gut feelings are often correct, and when reading a person, you should give credence to your gut feeling about the person. When studying a person and you get a feeling that the person is socially warm, you should entertain this profiling while analyzing the body language of the person. While taking gut feeling into account, you should classify it under subjective analysis as it is not based on observable traits and behaviors but on an inner feeling.

Furthermore, watch the eye contact. Establishing eye contact suggests eagerness and confidence in engaging the audience. Avoiding eye contact suggests stage fright and shyness as well as lack confidence in what one is talking about. A continued look is a stare, and it is intended to intimidate, or it may suggest absentmindedness of the individual.

If one continuously blinking eyes while looking at a target person suggests flirting behavior. An eye contact that gradually drops to the chest and thigh of the individual suggests a deviation of thoughts from the conversation. Eye contact is usually a dead giveaway when referring to potential lies and deception. Hence, paying attention to eye contact is an essential part of gaining a person's confidence.

Expectedly, pay attention to touch. The way one shakes hands speaks a lot about their confidence and formality. A firm handshake that is brief indicates confidence and professionalism.

A weak handshake that is brief indicates that one is feeling unease. On the other hand, a prolonged handshake, whether weak or strong, suggests that the person is trying to flirt with you, especially if it is between opposite sexes. Touching someone on the head may suggest rudeness.

Finally, listen to the tone of voice and laughter. Laughing may suggest happiness or sarcasm. Americans are good at manifesting sarcastically laughter, and it is attained by varying the tone of the laughter.

The tone of the voice tells about if the person is feeling confident and authoritative or not. In overall, a variation of tone implies that the individual is speaking naturally and convincingly. A flat tone indicates a lack of self-confidence and unfamiliarity with the conversation or audience.

Cold Reading: a means of getting to know people

A common tactic used to read people is cold reading. This tactic consists in making blanket statements in which you hope to hit the mark at some point. When you do hit a point, this can open the door for you to gain more information from your interlocutor. These are techniques which are used by psychics, fortune tellers and other types of mentalists who claim to read personalities on the spot.

When used correctly, you can extract great deals of information without actually having to ask. Here are a couple of techniques which you can put into effect.

- **The shotgun effect.** This effect consists in firing a large amount of small pellets of information. For example, you can observe someone's drooping shoulders and say, "I sense tension in you. Is something getting you down? Is work affection you? Are you stressed out about work?" You can even make observations such as "You must be stressed out about that traffic jam", or "the weather has been awful. I'm sure that must have you concerned".

These types of statements help make your interlocutors feel comfortable since you are incredibly perceptive. This tactic works so long as you are able to make enough observations to a point where one of them sticks to something that is real for that person.

- **The Forer effect.** In this tactic, you are making statements in which a person can go ahead and fill in the blanks. These statement are open-ended so that the individual can provide the information you need in order to complete your assessment. For example, a person who is visibly upset may react to a statement such as, "I can tell you are going through a lot". This is a clear signal to your interlocutor that your perceptive. While you are making a rather obvious observation, your interlocutor will feel comfortable to open up.

- **The rainbow.** This is a tactic similar to the the Forer effect. What this tactic does is make a blanket statement followed up by a rather obvious assumption. For instance, "you seem like a naturally upbeat person, but I get the sense that you have been through something tough lately". This statement combines an assumption with an observation that might seem insightful but is really intended to get the other person to open up and share details. Then, you can feed off those cues and expand on your observations.

As such, cold reading can help you make headway in getting to know a person. It will certainly help you to get others to warm up to you. If done right, you should be able to get other people to feel comfortable around you.

Activity

a. James is giving a speech. He starts by standing on one leg and brushes his unkempt hair. At first, his voice shakes before becoming natural and with varying tone. As the speech goes on, James initiates a continued stare at one of the audience members who is sleeping. Then James continues with the speech walking at half the stage.

When James looks at the watch after fifteen minutes, he suddenly speaks fast than he did and throws his hands randomly in the air. As a journalist covering the event for the first time and without prior knowledge of James read James.

b. Arnold finally meets the woman that they have been chatting on Facebook for over two months. When Arnold offers to shake the hand of the lady, she obliges but quickly withdraws her hand. Arnold then tries to initiate eye contact, to which the lady reciprocates by looking down.

When Arnold welcomes the lady to the public bench, she sits far from him. When Arnold asks the lady if she is unease and probably needs some time to make her mind if necessary to proceed with the date, she indicates that she is okay and that they should continue with the date. Read Arnold. Read the lady.

c. Pick any episode of any season of the TV series "The Big Bang Theory" and mute the volume of the TV or computer or smartphone. After watching the first 17 minutes, try to read the behavior of the participating characters based purely on their body language. Ensure that the episode does not have language subtitles.

Go ahead and repeat this for any movie or TV series you have to enhance your skill of reading people. The best experience is a movie or TV series that you are yet to watch.

Chapter 13:

How to Improve your People Reading Skills

One way of improving your people reading skills is to observe people in your daily life. Like any form of reading, one has to frequently engage in reading other people. The best starting point is the people close to you as you get to test the accuracy of your body language reading skills. For instance, observe your roommate's bodily cues and try to guess his or her emotional status.

Even though it might appear as spying on the person, you can go ahead and label the person as Specimen Y and maintain a journal of their non-verbal communication and what you concluded. When reading the body language of a person, the intention is not to judge them or correct them but to accurately determine how they are feeling without asking the individual verbally.

Focus more on people in groups as most try to mimic each other. Reading people in groups is important because in most cases, people are in social contexts where they are several people.

People in groups such as in a class, a stadium or workplace tend to mimic each other. If one person takes a selfie, chances are that the others will also take selfies. If one person starts taking a walk, chances are that the rest will also join inadvertently. It appears that when an individual is placed in a group setting, then he or she is likely to let others dictate how they act and react. In most cases, people will deliberately suppress undesired emotions and actions to accommodate others or simply fit in. Against this backdrop, reading people in a group can improve your effective body language reading competencies

Equally important, you should exhibit awareness. You should pay attention to everything that the person is doing and when the person is doing it. While this appears trivial, each small and subtle detail about the target person is necessary for one to accurately profile the person. For instance, if the target person adjusts earing, you should not assume that this is a mundane aspect and does not constitute body language. Being awake to every aspect of behavior, actions, and movements of the target person are critical to effectively reading the non-verbal cues of the individual. Awareness requires that you also understand yourself first, and this can be realized through emotional intelligence competencies.

For emphasis, study people you admire. Another way of attaining this is to find any recordings or videos of the people, mute the voice and study only the body language. With social media, people are sharing videos and audio recordings that one can learn from. You can also get a movie, especially the one that you are to watch, mute the volume, and analyze the non-verbal communication. Then get a paper and profile each of the characters observed on their personality and emotion. Once you have completed the profiling, activate the volume, and compare the perceived character against the cues that you have interpreted.

Another way is to read the body language is to connect with the person to determine the truthfulness of their emotions and personality. Try to mirror the target person by mimicking their body positions, matching their tone, and carrying the same pace of the conversation. When mimicking the individual, ensure that it is done in a subtle manner. Through mirroring, one creates a synergy and connection which enables you gets into the mind of the target person. Mimicking another person's bodily cues should be carefully done to avoid making it appear like you are trying to flirt or that you are creepy.

Look for additional cues when you encounter that the target person is crossing their arms and legs. Crossing the arms and legs denotes that one is defensive, but most people cross their arms and legs when feeling comfortable or if they want to concentrate more about what is being spoken.

If someone holds a drink on the table using the opposite hand, then the person is showing a lack of confidence. In overall, body language cues should be read as an entire set as focusing on one can be misleading. Where necessary, consider the cultural or learned behavior that may elicit a different meaning from what the non-verbal communication is suggesting. For instance, people that stammer may throw gestures randomly or stomp their feet, and this does not imply that they are lacking confidence or are scared.

Focus more on eye contact of the individual. You can initiate eye contact with the target person and observe their eye contact behavior. Eye contact, just like touch, communicates much more about the person and their emotional status. Staring at the ceiling or on the floor may indicate that the individual is bored and not interested in what is being said.

However, an individual may look on the floor or stare at the ceiling if the news being given is negative and painful such as the loss of a friend or loss of a job. In this context, avoiding eye contact does not imply that the individual is not listening, but instead, the person is thinking deeper about how to navigate the negative emotions. There are also extreme situations where eye contact can mislead, such as people that shy who will avoid eye contact.

Equally important is that you should watch for the shoulder posture of the target person to read their body language. If the person holds their shoulders by their ears, then it is a sign of tension and can make the speaker become unease as well. Relaxed shoulders indicate that one is feeling calm and alert. If the person tries to retract the shoulders closer to the trunk of the body as if an umbrella closing, then the person is feeling embarrassed or unease with the environment or the message being passed. Fortunately, the posture of the shoulders can be read from a distant position.

Another area that can help you improve body reading is the sitting posture of the individual. Slouching on the seat suggests casualness or tiredness of the target person. If the person spreads their legs wide while seated, then it indicates that the individual is not participating in the conversation.

Crossing the legs may indicate that the person is feeling unease or relaxed when participating in the conversation. It is important that you take note of the sitting posture of the target person as it communicates about the attitude and emotional status of the individual. It might be necessary to walk near the audience and take note of their sitting posture.

Like any form of reading, recognize and address personal bias and stereotypes. Each one of us has ingrained biases and stereotypes, which is largely a function of our parenting and environment. For instance, if you grew up in a strict Christian family, then you may show disdain to an atheist, and the contrary is true. There are visible attributes of a person that can trigger biases that will distract making an objective conclusion about the target individual.

For instance, the skin color or gender of the target person can distort the objective reading of the target individual. If you are a man and you notice that the target person, a woman is staring at the neighbor who is a man also then your biases may make you think they are in love because that is how you view women. It is important to recognize and work on personal biases to help you objectively profile the target person.

If there is an opportunity, study, and analyze the handshake or hug offered by the target person. When analyzing the handshake, try to assess it in combination with the facial expression exhibited. For instance, if you shake the hand of the other person and the person shakes your hand firmly but looks down then the person could be naturally shy, and this may imply that the person is confident as the one that shakes the hand firmly and maintains eye contact.

On the other hand, if you shake the hand of the person and the individual firmly shakes your hand but frowns, then the person could be feeling unease and irked by your previous behavior or comments.

Lastly, like any other form of reading competencies, it is necessary to prepare for reading people by going through resources that discuss and analyze communicative cues. For instance, get a book or presentation or documentaries on body language and study them. You can only analyze what you know at first. For instance, there several aspects of touch that people do not and will not take them into consideration when reading touch.

The same is true for posture and facial expressions. The more theoretical knowledge you have on body language, the more effective you will be at reading the non-verbal cues of people.

Activity

Search for TV series "Gary Unmarried" and pick one episode then focus on the character Dr. Walter Krandall who was Gary and Allison marriage counselor. Assess how effective he is in reading the body language of Gary and Allison.

Chapter 14:
How to Take Advantage of Reading People

Having gone through in what constitutes reading people, the role of body language, and how to read non-verbal communication, then it is important that one learns on ways of benefitting from reading the cues from people. In this context, the benefit realized from reading the body language of people is not to torment or use people but rather to enhance your interests that are acceptable such as increasing business deals.

First, reading help can help you win over a difficult customer or person. At one point, you have encountered a difficult person to understand and get along with despite the best of your efforts. Armed with people reading competencies, you can correctly analyze their tone, posture, touch, eye contact, and facial expressions to correctly connect with the individual.

For instance, using paralinguistic skills, you can strike a rapport with the person. Some customers are defensive, but if you are armed with people reading skills, then you will easily manage to manipulate them to your advantage. For instance, if you call a customer when he or she speaks in high-pitched voice, then probably the customer is angry or frustrated by workload or other life issues. Using this knowledge, you can use your voice pitch as a form of therapy to sound appealing to the customer and win them over.

Secondly, giving workers negative feedback about their weaknesses can be realized through reading body language. One of the most challenging undertakings is to give your partner or colleague negative feedback about their actions. Fortunately, people reading will enable you to get the right timing and offer a difficult message. Through body language, you will acknowledge any difficulties with processing the negative message by the target person. For instance, if you make a worker aware that he or she is not keeping time and he or she laughs, but the laughter is not natural, then you will conclude that the negative message was poorly processed by the person.

If you make an employee aware that their appraisal score is below average and he or she stares at the ground, then the individual is likely to be devastated by the news, and this implies that the message was either poorly delivered or poorly processed by the target person.

Thirdly, effective conflict resolution can be realized by reading the cues from the target person. Assuming that you are an arbiter in a conflict, you should read the non-verbal cues of the feuding parties to discover any shared ground and the emotive issues. Individuals will show panic, uneasiness, and stiffness when emotive issues are raised such as grinning, crossing arms, breathing fast and showing cold stare. Individuals will nod if something they agree to is mentioned.

They may also stamp their feet, clap hands, and shake hands to show a willingness to talk or strike a compromise. An arbiter will use people reading skills to identify hardliners and use body language to thaw the hard stance of such people. The participants themselves can also read the cues of the other party and appreciate their stance and make attempts to initiate meaningful conversation. All these combined efforts will give one an edge in solving conflicts.

Fourthly, improving the relationship with your partner can be attained by exploiting people reading competencies. Body language is critical in forming and sustaining social relationships as well as intimate relationships. If you have issues with relating with your partner, understanding and using touch can help understand how they feel.

Taking note of the facial expressions and tonal variation of your partner or the person you are talking to will help you understand and improve the relationship. The sitting posture of the target person can help one read and adjust their emotions and actions to the target person.

Think of now understanding what the facial expression of your partner means when previously you did not adequately process these messages. Your partner is likely to find you more listening and more affectionate. When one feels that he or she is being listened, cared for, and understood, then the individual is likely to feel loved and respected.

Fifthly, through reading people, one can improve the relationship with his or her children. Understanding a child and relating to it requires reading their body language and adjusting the interaction.

Children respond positively to affectionate touch, and a parent can hold their children affectionately to ease their worries. The physical distance between a child and a parent when speaking can help tell how it is feeling. For instance, if the child is unease to move closer to the parent, then chances are that the child is feeling worried that he or she has done something embarrassing or unethical.

Reluctance to stand closer or sit closer to a parent may also suggest abuse and a parent should read and validate this. A child that lowers the voice to almost a muffle may be feeling pain, isolated or uncared for. Using competencies of reading body language, a parent can increase their understanding of how a child is feeling because most children may not comprehensively manifest their feelings.

Sixthly, reading body language can help one make conversations interesting. We also would like to enliven conversations, but it is not always the case. One effective way to improve how other people perceive you is to understand their current status and adjust your words and non-verbal communication.

For instance, if you read the contextual cues of the other person and realize that he or she is feeling disinterested or exhausted; you can suggest a break or crack a joke. Through eye contact, you can make the other person feel recognized and wanted to join in the conversation. If the entire group or audience feels disinterested in the conversation by yawning, slouching on their chairs, crossing their legs and losing eye contact, then the speaker should conduct a quick self-feedback and adjust the communication. In this manner, taking advantage of people reading can make one an effective communicator.

Additionally, taking advantage of reading people can help one to recognize any dishonesty and pretense in a conversation. Focusing on verbal communication alone is not enough to accurately determine if one is pretending.

For instance, your child may say that he is comfortable going out to play while his body language suggests otherwise. For instance, the child could be replying in a high-pitched voice and laugh sarcastically that he or she is comfortable going out to play. The parent will use this body language to address the true feeling of the child.

In an intimate relationship, determining the true emotional status of your partner is critical for peaceful and constructive interaction. For instance, if your partner states that she believes you, but her voice is high-pitched, and she is throwing gestures randomly, then chances are that she is not, and in fact, she is angry at you.

Equally important is that exploiting people reading can make one make a good first impression. A good first impression is critical when selling, during an interview, and when seeking a life partner. Armed with reading non-verbal communication one can deliberately enhance positive non-verbal cues such as nodding to a speech, using gestures when necessary and speaking in a low-pitched voice to sound professional.

When one feels tired and wants to shuffle feet or lower eye contact, one can compensate for that by interrupting the speaker to ask a question or take notes. Expectedly, one will offer a firm handshake and accompany it with a smile. Making a good first impression can improve and open opportunities for you in the case of negotiation, interviews, making sales, and seeking a marriage partner.

Relatedly, exploiting people reading skills can improve performance during interviews and press conferences. The first way is that one can predict who the ideal communicator is an exhibit the expected communication skills.

For instance, appearing calm, using a reassuring voice, and maintaining eye contact will make the journalists covering the press conference treat what you are saying authoritative and truthful. The second way is that the person giving the interview can read the contextual clues of the audience and journalists and ascertain their emotional status and adjust the verbal communication and body language to give a corporate response.

For instance, if the body language of the audience or journalists suggest that they are doubting what you said earlier, then the speaker should act and speak with authority, composure and match with effective gestures and facial expressions. The overall goal of exploiting people reading skills during interviews and press conferences is to sound professional and convincing.

Additionally, taking advantage of the people reading can help one to correctly identify issues in a relationship by analyzing body language. Apart from just reading the contextual clues and improving social and intimate relationships, one can also use reading people skills to determine the presence of issues in relationships.

For instance, you might notice that when you introduce talk on certain issues with your partner, their non-verbal communication suggests defensiveness and anger. For this reason, reading people can help get to the underlying issue even in cases where the partner is determined not to open up.

Using body language to identify issues can also help a parent to determine what is bothering a child in cases where the child retreats to its world. The parent can try talking over general issues as well as specific issues and watch the body language of the child to guess the likely issue bothering it.

Similarly, effectively teaching or sharing ideas can be enhanced by reading the body language of the target audience. For instance, a teacher can improve understanding of the students by taking note of signs of lack of concentration such as yawning or staring at the ceiling. At the same time, the teacher can adjust their non-verbal cues to avoid distracting the students from the main message.

Just like verbal communication, non-verbal communication can also contain noise where the non-verbal cues of communication distort the intended message. Outside the teaching context, one can improve on sharing ideas by reading the body language of the audience and evoking the desired emotion and reaction. For instance, one should ensure that the target audience is relaxed and alert by evaluating the sitting posture, eye contact, and facial expressions before starting a presentation. Sharing ideas effectively depends on accurate timing and actors; orators and politicians understand this well.

Finally, taking advantage of reading body language will lead to improved emotional intelligence and social skills to make one more appealing and understanding. Emotional intelligence involves being aware of how you feel and also acknowledging how others feel to enhance mutual understanding.

For this reason, non-verbal communication is a critical avenue to read the emotional status of the other person. Emotional intelligence requires correctly reading the emotional status of an individual to enable you to empathize with how they feel. Against this backdrop, reading the contextual clues of a target audience gives an added advantage to an individual to evoke and apply social skills as well as understand self-deeper.

Think of speaking to a colleague and manifesting non-verbal cues that you are offended, but the person is not registering what you are feeling. In this context, effective communication will not only be hampered, but the social relationship will also be affected negatively.

Activity

a. Watch the movie "The Wolf street" and observe how body language is used to enhance sales.

b. Watch the movie "Get Hard" with lead actor Kevin Hart and assess if the hand gestures align with verbal communication. If possible watch the entire movie and note the gestures and facial expressions exhibited when one is angry. Do you think the movie used too much body language than necessary? What do you learn from this movie with respect to body language?

Conclusion

In conclusion, the book walked the reader through an introduction to human behavior, types of body language, and how to exploit people reading skills in order to analyze people. The book offered an activity that the reader should find interesting and relevant to help understand non-verbal communication deeper. a common misconception by most people is that they know body language and therefore see no need to read, practice, and apply it.

Armed with this understanding, the author presented relatable real-life examples and ensured the simplicity and flow of content and chapters. The read will find the chapters and content connected, which help builds the understanding. The book also employs simple language, making it a ready across speakers of the English language with different mastery of the language.

Relatedly, the author assumed that the reader has no prior knowledge of analyzing people and presented the content with an informative and authoritative manner. The book is nonjudgmental and standard, making it a preferable read to different cadres of readers. The examples and activities used are free of biases.

As the book concluded, the reader is now assumed to be ready to apply what has been discussed systematically. Using an innovative approach, the book used movie characters and certain public figures to help the reader appreciate the real-life application of people reading and exhibiting appropriate body language. For the best experience, the reader should read the chapters systematically as the content is related and develops gradually.